Microservices Architecture: Design, Deployment, and Management

James Relington

DEDICATION

To those who seek knowledge, inspiration, and new perspectives—
may this book be a companion on your journey, a spark for curiosity,
and a reminder that every page turned is a step toward discovery.

AKNOWLEDGEMENTS

I would like to express my deepest gratitude to everyone who contributed to the creation of this book. To my colleagues and mentors, your insights and expertise have been invaluable. A special thank you to my family and friends for their unwavering support and encouragement throughout this journey.

Introduction to Microservices Architecture

Microservices architecture represents a significant shift from traditional monolithic application design. In a monolithic system, all components of the application are tightly integrated into a single, indivisible unit. This approach can be simple to develop and deploy initially but becomes increasingly difficult to scale and maintain as the application grows. The limitations of monolithic architecture, particularly in handling large-scale applications, have led to the rise of microservices as a more flexible, scalable, and maintainable solution. Microservices architecture advocates for breaking down an application into a collection of small, loosely coupled services, each responsible for a specific business function.

The key characteristic of microservices is their modularity. Unlike monolithic systems, which operate as a single block, microservices are independently deployable services that interact with one another via well-defined APIs. Each microservice is designed to perform a specific function or set of related tasks, and these services can be developed, deployed, and scaled independently. This independent nature allows development teams to work more efficiently, as they can focus on smaller, manageable sections of the application without being concerned about the entire system.

A typical microservices architecture consists of a variety of independent services, each often based on different technologies. For example, one service might be written in Java, while another might be written in Python or Node.js. These services communicate with one another using lightweight protocols such as HTTP or messaging queues. This contrasts with monolithic systems, where the entire application is often built using a single technology stack. By decoupling services and allowing them to communicate over the network, microservices promote flexibility in terms of technology choices and scaling strategies.

The autonomy of each service in a microservices architecture provides several benefits. It allows teams to choose the best technology stack for each individual service based on its specific needs. For example, a service that requires high-performance processing might be built using a low-level programming language like C++, while a service that deals with user interactions might be better suited to a higher-level language like JavaScript. Additionally, microservices can be deployed in isolation, which helps avoid the dependency and versioning issues common in monolithic systems.

Microservices also support continuous delivery and DevOps practices. Since each service can be deployed independently, development teams can iterate on specific services without disrupting the entire application. This enables faster release cycles, which is critical in today's competitive software landscape. Continuous integration and deployment (CI/CD) pipelines become more effective in a microservices environment, as each service can be built, tested, and deployed independently, without waiting for other services to be ready. This autonomy accelerates development and reduces the time to market for new features or bug fixes.

One of the main advantages of microservices is their ability to scale more effectively than monolithic applications. In a monolithic system, scaling typically means replicating the entire application, which can be inefficient and resource-intensive. In contrast, with microservices, scaling is more granular. Individual services can be scaled independently based on demand, allowing for more efficient use of resources. If a particular service experiences heavy load, it can be scaled up, while other services that are not under pressure can remain at their current scale. This results in better resource utilization and cost savings, particularly in cloud environments where infrastructure costs are based on usage.

While microservices offer significant advantages in terms of scalability and flexibility, they also introduce new complexities. One of the key challenges in microservices architecture is managing communication between the services. Since each service is independent, they need to communicate over a network, which can introduce latency and other performance issues. Developers need to carefully design the communication protocols between services to ensure they are reliable, efficient, and fault-tolerant. Tools like API gateways, service discovery mechanisms, and message brokers help manage service communication, but they also add additional layers of complexity that must be managed effectively.

Another challenge is ensuring data consistency in a distributed environment. In a monolithic system, the database is often shared among all components, making it easier to maintain consistency. In a microservices system, each service typically has its own database, which can lead to challenges in maintaining data consistency and handling transactions that span multiple services. Techniques like eventual consistency, event sourcing, and the Saga pattern are commonly used to manage these challenges, but they require careful consideration and design.

Security is another important concern in microservices architecture. Each service is a potential point of vulnerability, and with many independent services interacting with each other, the attack surface is significantly larger than in a monolithic system. It is essential to implement security measures such as authentication and authorization at the service level, as well as encryption for data in transit and at rest. Additionally, centralized logging and monitoring systems are critical to detecting and responding to security incidents in a timely manner.

Despite these challenges, microservices have proven to be a powerful architecture pattern, especially for organizations looking to build large-scale, flexible, and maintainable systems. The ability to develop, deploy, and scale services independently makes microservices an ideal choice for applications that need to evolve quickly and support frequent releases. This is particularly true for organizations adopting cloud-native architectures, where microservices can be combined with containerization and orchestration tools like Docker and Kubernetes to further streamline development and deployment processes.

In conclusion, microservices architecture offers a modern, scalable, and flexible approach to building software applications. By breaking down an application into smaller, independently deployable services, organizations can enjoy improved scalability, faster development cycles, and greater flexibility in technology choices. However, the complexities of managing distributed systems, communication, data consistency, and security must be carefully addressed. With the right tools and practices in place, microservices can offer significant advantages over traditional monolithic architectures, enabling organizations to build more resilient and efficient systems.

Key Principles of Microservices Design

The design of microservices architecture is grounded in several key principles that are essential for creating a robust, scalable, and maintainable system. These principles guide the structuring of the application, ensuring that the microservices are not only functional but also efficient, resilient, and adaptable to change. While there is no one-size-fits-all approach to microservices design, several common principles can be applied to most systems to achieve the desired outcomes. These principles focus on modularity, scalability, flexibility, and independent deployability, all of which are central to the effectiveness of microservices.

One of the most fundamental principles of microservices design is the concept of bounded contexts. A bounded context refers to the explicit boundaries that define the responsibility and scope of a service. Each microservice is designed to handle a specific business function, and these functions are isolated from one another. This ensures that each service operates independently and has a clear purpose, making it easier to understand, develop, and maintain. Bounded contexts also help avoid tight coupling between services, which can lead to a monolithic structure that defeats the purpose of adopting microservices in the first place. By establishing these boundaries, the microservices can evolve independently, allowing teams to focus on individual components without worrying about the entire system.

Another key principle is the notion of loose coupling between services. Microservices should be designed to communicate with one another through well-defined interfaces, such as APIs or messaging queues, and should not have direct dependencies on each other's internal logic or data. This loose coupling ensures that each service can be developed, deployed, and scaled independently. Changes made to one service should not require changes to others, which is one of the primary advantages of microservices over monolithic architectures. Loose coupling not only makes development more efficient but also improves the resilience of the system. If one service fails, it does not bring down the entire system, allowing other services to continue functioning without disruption.

Independence is another key design principle that underpins microservices architecture. Each microservice should be capable of being developed, deployed, and scaled independently of the others. This allows development teams to work on separate services simultaneously without having to coordinate with other teams constantly. The independent nature of microservices is particularly advantageous in large teams, as different teams can take ownership of different services, improving productivity and reducing bottlenecks. Moreover, it enables continuous deployment practices, as new versions of individual services can be deployed without impacting the rest of the system. This independence also supports rapid iteration and experimentation, which is vital in a fast-paced development environment where businesses need to adapt quickly to changing requirements.

A key principle related to independence is the use of decentralized data management. In a monolithic application, there is typically a single database that serves the entire system. In contrast, microservices each have their own data store, which allows them to manage their data independently. This decentralized approach to data management ensures that each service can optimize its data storage and retrieval mechanisms according to its specific requirements. It also prevents services from becoming tightly coupled to a central database, reducing the risk of bottlenecks and improving the overall performance and scalability of the system. However, decentralized data management introduces challenges in maintaining data consistency across services, which requires careful consideration and design of techniques such as eventual consistency or the Saga pattern.

Another essential design principle is the emphasis on resiliency and fault tolerance. Microservices should be designed to withstand failure and continue functioning even if one or more services experience issues. This can be achieved through techniques such as circuit breakers, retries, and fallback mechanisms. By building resilience into the design of each service, the system as a whole can maintain high availability, even in the event of partial failures. This is especially important in large-scale distributed systems, where the likelihood of failure increases due to the complexity of the system and the number of interacting components. The ability to gracefully handle failure is one of the key benefits of microservices over monolithic systems, which often fail as a whole when a single component experiences issues.

Scalability is another crucial principle of microservices design. A primary advantage of microservices is the ability to scale individual services independently, based on their specific demands. For example, if one service is handling a large volume of traffic while others are not, it can be scaled up without affecting the performance of the rest of the system. This ability to scale horizontally, by adding more instances of a specific service, is particularly valuable in cloud environments, where resources are often dynamically allocated. By allowing each service to scale independently, microservices architecture provides more efficient resource utilization and can better accommodate fluctuating workloads.

Microservices should also be designed to support automation and continuous integration/continuous deployment (CI/CD) pipelines. The modularity and independence of microservices lend themselves well to automated testing, deployment, and monitoring. Each service can be tested and deployed independently, which simplifies the development process and accelerates time-to-market. Automation also reduces the potential for human error, ensuring that new versions of services are deployed consistently and reliably. A robust CI/CD pipeline allows teams to continuously deliver updates to individual services, enabling rapid innovation and minimizing downtime.

Security is an often-overlooked but essential aspect of microservices design. Given the distributed nature of microservices, each service can potentially be a target for security threats. Therefore, it is crucial to implement security measures at both the service level and the communication level. Authentication and authorization mechanisms should be implemented within each service to ensure that only authorized users or services can access the data or functionality. Additionally, secure communication channels, such as HTTPS or encrypted messaging, should be used to protect data in transit. Centralized monitoring and logging can help detect potential security incidents, but security should be built into the design of each service from the outset.

Lastly, observability is a key principle in microservices design. Since microservices are distributed across multiple services, monitoring and troubleshooting can become more complex than in monolithic systems. To address this, microservices should be designed with built-in observability features, such as logging, metrics collection, and tracing. These features enable teams to track the performance and health of each service, detect potential issues early, and respond quickly to problems. Distributed tracing, for example, allows developers to track requests as they move through different services, helping to pinpoint bottlenecks and identify areas for optimization.

In summary, designing microservices architecture requires a deep understanding of key principles such as bounded contexts, loose coupling, independence, decentralized data management, resiliency, scalability, automation, security, and observability. By adhering to these principles, organizations can build systems that are flexible, scalable, and maintainable, while also enabling rapid development and deployment cycles. However, it is important to recognize that microservices architecture is not a one-size-fits-all solution, and the application of these principles must be carefully tailored to meet the unique needs and challenges of each system.

Building Blocks of Microservices Systems

The building blocks of microservices systems form the foundation upon which the architecture is structured. These essential components work together to ensure that microservices can function independently, scale effectively, and remain resilient. While microservices architecture allows for flexibility and autonomy in service development and deployment, certain core building blocks are necessary to achieve the desired functionality. These blocks help maintain loose coupling between services, ensure efficient communication, and provide mechanisms for managing data and security. Understanding these fundamental components is critical for designing robust microservices systems that can adapt to the dynamic needs of modern software applications.

One of the primary building blocks of microservices is the service itself. Each microservice is designed to handle a specific business function, such as processing orders, managing customer information, or handling payments. The service is the smallest unit of functionality that is independently deployable and scalable. It interacts with other services through well-defined interfaces, such as RESTful APIs, which allow it to communicate with the rest of the system. These services are typically designed to be loosely coupled, meaning that changes in one service should not affect the others. This independence is crucial for maintaining agility in development, as teams can work on different services concurrently without worrying about disrupting the entire application.

Another key building block is the database. In a monolithic system, a single database is often shared by all components of the application. However, in microservices architecture, each service typically has its own database or data store, allowing it to manage its data independently. This approach, known as decentralized data management, ensures that each service can choose the most appropriate database technology for its needs, such as a relational database, a NoSQL database, or a time-series database. By decoupling data management from other services, microservices avoid the performance bottlenecks and scalability limitations that can occur when all components rely on a single, centralized database. This also allows for more flexible and efficient scaling of individual services based on their data usage patterns.

Communication between services is another critical building block in microservices systems. Since microservices are distributed across different servers or containers, they must communicate over a network. This communication can be synchronous, using protocols such as HTTP or gRPC, or asynchronous, using message brokers like RabbitMQ or Kafka. Synchronous communication is often used when one service needs immediate data or processing from another, while asynchronous communication is typically used for events or background tasks. The choice of communication protocol depends on the specific needs of the services and the overall system design. It is essential to ensure that communication between services is efficient, reliable, and scalable, as delays or failures in service communication can disrupt the entire system.

Service discovery is another key building block in a microservices architecture. As microservices are often deployed in dynamic environments, such as cloud platforms or container orchestration systems like Kubernetes, their locations and endpoints can change frequently. Service discovery enables services to locate each other automatically, ensuring that they can communicate without the need for manual configuration. This process typically involves a service registry, where each service registers itself upon startup and periodically updates its status. Other services can then query the registry to find the correct location of the service they need to interact with. Service discovery is a critical component in large-scale systems where the number of services can grow rapidly, making manual management of service locations impractical.

API gateways are another essential building block in microservices systems. An API gateway acts as a single entry point for all client requests, routing them to the appropriate microservices based on the request type. It provides a centralized layer that can handle cross-cutting concerns such as authentication, authorization, logging, rate limiting, and caching. By consolidating these concerns in a single gateway, microservices can focus on their core business logic without needing to implement these functions individually. The API gateway can also provide load balancing, ensuring that requests are distributed evenly across the available instances of each microservice. This helps to optimize resource usage and improve the overall performance of the system.

A related building block is the concept of a service mesh. A service mesh is an infrastructure layer that manages the communication between microservices. It handles the complex tasks of load balancing, service discovery, and failure recovery, as well as providing observability and security features such as encryption and authentication. Service meshes typically use sidecar proxies that are deployed alongside each service instance to intercept and manage traffic. This allows developers to focus on building business logic while the service mesh handles the lower-level concerns of communication and security. Popular service mesh technologies include Istio and Linkerd, both of which provide powerful tools for managing microservices in large-scale distributed environments.

Another important building block in microservices systems is containerization. Microservices are often deployed in containers, which provide a lightweight and consistent runtime environment for services. Containers ensure that services can run in any environment, from a developer's local machine to a cloud platform, without worrying about inconsistencies in the underlying infrastructure. Docker is the most widely used containerization platform, and it allows microservices to be packaged with all their dependencies, ensuring that they can be executed reliably across different environments. Container orchestration platforms like Kubernetes are commonly used to manage the deployment, scaling, and operation of containers in production environments. Kubernetes provides automated scheduling, scaling, and self-healing, ensuring that services are always running and available, even in the face of failures.

Monitoring and logging are crucial building blocks for managing the health and performance of microservices systems. Given the distributed nature of microservices, traditional monitoring and logging tools are often insufficient. To address this, microservices require specialized tools that can provide end-to-end visibility across the entire system. Distributed tracing is an essential technique for tracking requests as they pass through different services, allowing developers to pinpoint bottlenecks and performance issues. Centralized logging solutions, such as the ELK stack (Elasticsearch, Logstash, and Kibana), aggregate logs from all services into a single repository, making it easier to analyze and troubleshoot issues. Metrics collection, through tools like Prometheus, provides insights into the performance and health of services, helping teams monitor the system's overall behavior and detect potential issues before they escalate.

Security is an integral part of the building blocks in microservices systems. Each service is a potential attack surface, and securing these services is critical to protecting sensitive data and maintaining the integrity of the system. Authentication and authorization mechanisms, such as OAuth and JWT, are commonly used to ensure that only authorized users and services can access the data and functionality provided by each microservice. Additionally, secure communication protocols like HTTPS should be used to encrypt data in transit, preventing unauthorized access to sensitive information. Centralized security management tools can help enforce security policies across all services, ensuring that each service adheres to the same security standards.

In a microservices architecture, data consistency can be a challenge, particularly when services have their own databases. The concept of eventual consistency is often employed, meaning that the system allows for temporary inconsistencies between services, which are resolved over time. Event sourcing and the Saga pattern are two techniques used to ensure data consistency across distributed services. Event sourcing involves capturing state changes as a sequence of events, while the Saga pattern breaks long-running transactions into smaller, manageable steps, each of which is handled by a different service.

These building blocks work together to create a cohesive and efficient microservices system. By focusing on the independence and autonomy of each service, while ensuring that communication, data management, security, and scalability are properly addressed, organizations can design microservices architectures that are resilient, flexible, and capable of supporting complex, large-scale applications. The integration of these blocks allows microservices to deliver the benefits of modularity, agility, and continuous delivery, making them a powerful approach for building modern software systems.

Designing Scalable Microservices

Designing scalable microservices requires a deep understanding of how applications behave under varying loads and how individual components of a system can grow and adapt to meet those demands. Scalability is one of the main benefits of microservices architecture, enabling organizations to handle increasing traffic, data volume, and complexity without compromising performance. Achieving scalability in microservices involves considering not only how services can be horizontally scaled but also how the system can be designed to efficiently manage resources, optimize performance, and ensure that each service can grow independently. As the demand on a system increases, microservices should be able to maintain or improve their responsiveness and reliability, without significant changes to the underlying architecture.

The first step in designing scalable microservices is to ensure that each service is stateless. Statelessness is a fundamental design principle that facilitates scaling. When a service is stateless, it does not store any information about previous interactions, and each request is treated as independent. This means that services do not need to rely on in-memory data or local state to process requests, making it easier to add new instances of a service as demand increases. Stateless services can be scaled horizontally by simply adding more instances or containers without the need for synchronization or complex state management between instances. This approach makes scaling more efficient and reduces the risk of bottlenecks caused by services that are tightly coupled to their state.

Once services are designed to be stateless, the next consideration is how to manage service discovery. In a scalable microservices system, the number of service instances can fluctuate dynamically, especially in cloud-native environments where services may be spun up or down based on demand. Service discovery mechanisms are essential for ensuring that services can locate each other and communicate, even as their instances change. In Kubernetes, for instance, the dynamic nature of containerized services requires a service discovery solution that can automatically track the location of available instances. This process is typically managed through service registries that allow services to register themselves and be discovered by other services as needed. This dynamic discovery is critical to maintaining the scalability of the system, as it enables the addition or removal of services without disrupting the overall flow of communication.

Another key aspect of scalable microservices design is the use of load balancing. As the number of service instances increases, it becomes crucial to distribute incoming requests evenly across all available instances to prevent any single instance from becoming overwhelmed. Load balancing can be implemented at various levels, from the API gateway to the service level itself. An API gateway acts as a reverse proxy, distributing incoming requests to the appropriate microservice instances based on factors such as round-robin distribution or least-connections. Additionally, service meshes, which are becoming increasingly popular in microservices architectures, provide advanced load balancing features that can handle more complex scenarios, such as traffic splitting for canary releases or dynamic rerouting in the case of service failures. Proper load balancing ensures that no single service instance becomes a bottleneck, improving the responsiveness and reliability of the system.

When designing scalable microservices, it is important to also consider data management. In a monolithic system, a single database often serves as the central repository for all data. However, in a microservices architecture, each service typically manages its own data store. This decentralized approach to data management is essential for scaling individual services independently, but it introduces the challenge of ensuring data consistency across multiple databases. There are several strategies for managing data in a scalable microservices environment. One approach is event sourcing, where changes to the system state are captured as a sequence of events, allowing services to reconstruct the state of their databases at any point in time. Another approach is eventual consistency, where services asynchronously synchronize data and allow for temporary inconsistencies that will eventually be resolved. Both of these methods enable services to operate independently, ensuring that scalability is not compromised by data synchronization or locking issues.

As the system scales, monitoring and observability become increasingly critical. Without effective monitoring, it can be difficult to identify performance bottlenecks or understand how services are interacting with one another. Scalable microservices must be designed with observability in mind, allowing teams to collect metrics, logs, and traces that provide insight into the behavior of individual services. Distributed tracing is particularly important in microservices environments because it allows developers to track requests as they traverse multiple services. This helps identify performance bottlenecks and areas where optimization is needed. Tools such as Prometheus, Grafana, and the ELK stack are commonly used to gather and visualize metrics and logs from microservices. A robust monitoring system provides visibility into the health and performance of the system, enabling proactive management and quick resolution of issues that could impact scalability.

Another important consideration when designing scalable microservices is the handling of failures. In a distributed system, failures are inevitable, and it is essential to design microservices with fault tolerance in mind. One approach to improving the resilience of microservices is the use of circuit breakers. A circuit breaker prevents a service from making repeated requests to a failing service, allowing the system to degrade gracefully and recover without causing a cascade of failures. Additionally, techniques such as retries, backoff strategies, and fallback mechanisms can help services continue functioning in the face of temporary issues. By implementing fault tolerance mechanisms, microservices systems can maintain availability and performance even when individual components fail.

Autoscaling is another important factor in ensuring that microservices can scale effectively. In cloud environments, resources can be dynamically allocated based on the current load. Autoscaling allows services to automatically scale up or down in response to changes in traffic, ensuring that the system has the resources it needs to handle peak loads without over-provisioning. Kubernetes, for example, supports horizontal pod autoscaling, which adjusts the number of pod replicas based on CPU or memory usage. Autoscaling ensures that the system remains responsive and cost-effective by matching resource allocation to actual demand.

In addition to scalability, it is essential to design microservices for high availability. High availability ensures that services are accessible and functional even in the event of hardware or software failures. To achieve high availability, services should be deployed across multiple availability zones or regions to mitigate the impact of a failure in a single location. Replication and redundancy are key techniques for achieving high availability, as they ensure that there are backup instances of services that can take over in the event of a failure. Load balancers can then route traffic to healthy instances, ensuring minimal downtime and disruption to users.

Finally, when designing scalable microservices, it is essential to plan for future growth. A scalable system should be designed not only to handle current traffic but also to accommodate future increases in load. This involves anticipating potential bottlenecks and ensuring that services can be easily scaled and optimized as the system grows. It also requires a flexible and adaptable architecture that can evolve to meet new business needs and technological advances. By anticipating growth and planning for scalability from the outset, organizations can ensure that their microservices systems remain robust and capable of handling increasing demands over time.

The design of scalable microservices is a complex but rewarding process that involves considering many factors, including statelessness, load balancing, service discovery, data management, monitoring, fault tolerance, autoscaling, and high availability. When these elements are properly implemented, microservices can handle large-scale applications and dynamic workloads, ensuring that the system remains responsive, resilient, and cost-efficient as it grows. By focusing on scalability from the beginning, organizations can build microservices architectures that are capable of supporting both current and future business requirements.

Decomposition Strategies for Microservices

Decomposing an application into microservices is one of the most critical decisions in the design of a microservices-based system. The way in which a monolithic application is broken down into smaller, independent services can significantly impact the performance, scalability, and maintainability of the final system. Decomposition is not a one-size-fits-all approach, and there are several strategies to consider. The right strategy for decomposition depends on factors such as business requirements, team structure, technology stack, and existing system architecture. Each strategy has its own set of challenges and benefits, but the goal is always to create manageable, independently deployable services that allow the application to scale, evolve, and integrate with ease.

A common decomposition strategy is to break the application into services based on business capabilities. This approach involves identifying the distinct business functions or domains within the application and organizing services around them. Each service is designed to handle a specific business function, such as customer management, order processing, or inventory tracking. This type of decomposition is highly aligned with the domain-driven design (DDD) approach, which emphasizes dividing a system based on the different areas of expertise within the business. The key advantage of this strategy is that it ensures the system is organized around the needs of the business, and each service is responsible for a clear, well-defined function. It also allows for flexibility, as different teams can focus on different business domains, enabling parallel development and scaling efforts.

While business capability decomposition is effective for many applications, it is not always straightforward. Some business functions may be more complex than others, requiring additional decomposition into smaller services. For example, an order processing service may need to be split further into services that handle payments, shipping, and returns. Determining the right level of decomposition for each business domain requires a deep understanding of the business requirements and how services interact with one another. This strategy also introduces challenges related to managing data across multiple services, as each service will need its own data store to maintain autonomy. Ensuring data consistency while maintaining service independence is an important consideration when following this decomposition strategy.

Another strategy for decomposition is to base it on the system's technical layers. This approach involves splitting the application into services according to technical components, such as the user interface, application logic, and data access layers. For example, the user interface (UI) could be a separate service from the backend logic, which might in turn be broken down into separate services for data storage, messaging, or external API integrations. This type of decomposition is more focused on the technical architecture of the system rather than business logic, and it works well in cases where the application is already structured in a way that mirrors these layers. The benefit of this approach is that it provides a clear separation of concerns, with each service being responsible for a specific aspect of the system's functionality.

However, technical decomposition can sometimes create challenges related to the coordination of services that span multiple layers. For example, changes to the UI service may require updates to the backend logic or the data access layer. If these layers are decomposed into separate microservices, managing these interdependencies can become complex. Additionally, technical decomposition does not always align with business needs, which can make it difficult to prioritize work based on business objectives. The success of this strategy depends on a clear understanding of the system's architecture and the ability to effectively manage dependencies between services at different layers.

Decomposition based on the types of interactions between services is another viable strategy. In this case, services are organized according to the way they interact with each other and the external environment. For example, one service could handle synchronous communication with external systems, while another might handle asynchronous communication through event-driven mechanisms. This approach allows services to be designed around the communication patterns that are most appropriate for their function. For example, services that require real-time data could be designed to handle direct requests using synchronous protocols like REST or gRPC, while other services that process large volumes of data in the background could use message queues or event streams for asynchronous communication.

The benefit of this strategy is that it can optimize performance based on the communication model used by each service. For example, synchronous services can be optimized for low latency, while asynchronous services can be designed to handle high throughput and eventual consistency. However, one challenge with this approach is ensuring that the overall system remains cohesive despite the varying communication patterns. Coordination between services that use different communication models can become complicated, especially when handling failure scenarios or ensuring that data flows seamlessly across services. Additionally, services that rely on asynchronous communication need to be designed with eventual consistency in mind, which introduces its own set of challenges.

A more advanced decomposition strategy involves the use of the Strangler Pattern. This approach is often employed when transitioning from a monolithic application to a microservices architecture. The Strangler Pattern involves incrementally replacing the monolithic application with microservices, starting with one feature or component at a time. As new services are developed, they gradually replace the functionality of the monolith, "strangling" the old system until it is completely replaced. This strategy allows for a smooth migration from a monolithic to a microservices architecture, minimizing risk and ensuring that the system remains functional throughout the transition. The key advantage of the Strangler Pattern is that it allows for incremental progress and avoids the need for a large, risky rewrite of the entire application.

While the Strangler Pattern is an effective way to transition to microservices, it does introduce challenges related to managing both the monolithic and microservices components simultaneously. Ensuring that the new microservices integrate seamlessly with the old monolithic system can be complex, and careful planning is required to manage the dependencies between the two. Additionally, the Strangler Pattern relies on the ability to clearly identify the boundaries of the monolithic application's functionality, which may not always be straightforward. The success of this strategy depends on the organization's ability to manage the complexity of both architectures during the transition period.

When considering decomposition strategies, it is also important to evaluate how services will evolve over time. As business requirements change or new technologies are introduced, services may need to be refactored or redesigned. A strategy that is well-suited to current needs may become cumbersome as the system grows and evolves. Thus, decomposition should be approached with an understanding of how services will interact and change in the future. In many cases, the best strategy is a combination of approaches, such as decomposing services based on business capabilities but also considering communication patterns or technical layers to ensure scalability and maintainability.

Regardless of the strategy chosen, effective service boundaries are essential for successful decomposition. Identifying clear boundaries between services ensures that each microservice can evolve independently and minimizes the risk of creating tightly coupled components. Service boundaries should be based on factors such as functionality, data ownership, and communication patterns, and should take into account the organizational structure and team responsibilities. Well-defined service boundaries help ensure that each service can be developed, deployed, and maintained independently, which is essential for achieving the full benefits of a microservices architecture.

Choosing the right decomposition strategy for microservices is a complex but essential step in designing an effective microservices system. By focusing on business domains, technical layers, communication patterns, or incremental migration strategies, organizations can break down their applications into manageable, independently deployable services. The key to successful decomposition lies in understanding the needs of the business, the architecture of the system, and the long-term goals of the organization, ensuring that microservices are structured in a way that supports scalability, maintainability, and flexibility.

Microservices and the Single Responsibility Principle

The Single Responsibility Principle (SRP) is one of the most fundamental concepts in software design. It is one of the five SOLID principles, which are widely regarded as best practices for creating maintainable and scalable software. The essence of SRP is simple: a class or a service should have only one reason to change, meaning it should only be responsible for a single part of the system's functionality. This principle is highly applicable in the context of microservices architecture, where the goal is to break down an application into smaller, manageable services that can evolve independently. Adhering to the Single Responsibility Principle when designing microservices not only simplifies development but also leads to systems that are easier to maintain, scale, and deploy.

In a microservices architecture, each service is designed to fulfill a specific business function or capability. This aligns perfectly with the SRP because it ensures that every microservice has a clear, focused responsibility. For example, a microservice responsible for managing user accounts should not be concerned with processing payments or sending emails. Each service operates independently and encapsulates a single business capability, making it easier to understand, test, and modify. This contrasts sharply with monolithic architectures, where large, interconnected components often share responsibilities and have overlapping concerns, making them harder to manage and scale. The decomposition into microservices allows teams to focus on one responsibility at a time, reducing complexity and improving the overall clarity of the system.

One of the primary advantages of adhering to the Single Responsibility Principle in microservices design is the ability to improve maintainability. When a service is responsible for just one task, understanding its purpose and functionality becomes straightforward. Development teams can work on isolated services without needing to navigate through unrelated functionality. This separation of concerns also reduces the risk of introducing bugs. For example, if a bug is found in a service that manages customer data, developers can quickly trace the problem to that specific service, without having to dig through the entire codebase. Furthermore, making changes to a single, well-defined responsibility is less likely to have unintended consequences on other parts of the system. This simplifies debugging and minimizes the impact of updates.

The SRP also helps in creating a system that is easier to scale. Microservices that adhere to the principle of single responsibility can be scaled independently, which is one of the core benefits of the architecture. If one particular business function experiences increased demand, only the microservice responsible for that function needs to be scaled, rather than the entire monolithic application. For example, if a microservice handling payment processing becomes a bottleneck, additional instances of this service can be deployed to handle the increased load, without affecting other services such as user authentication or inventory management. This fine-grained control over scaling ensures that resources are utilized efficiently, which is especially important in cloud-based environments where cost is often tied to resource usage.

The SRP also plays a crucial role in simplifying deployment and release cycles. When services are designed with a single responsibility, they are decoupled from other services and can be deployed independently. This independence makes it easier to implement continuous delivery and integration pipelines, as new versions of a service can be deployed without affecting others. For example, if a microservice that manages product catalog data needs an update, it can be deployed on its own, without requiring a complete redeployment of the entire application. This reduces downtime, minimizes the risk of deployment failures, and accelerates time to market for new features or bug fixes. Additionally, this level of independence fosters a culture of continuous improvement, as each service can evolve at its own pace, driven by the specific needs of the business.

While adhering to SRP in microservices design offers many benefits, it is not without challenges. One of the primary challenges is defining the boundaries of responsibility for each service. If a service is too granular, it can lead to an excessive number of services, each requiring its own deployment pipeline, monitoring, and maintenance. On the other hand, if services are too broad, they may violate SRP by taking on multiple responsibilities, which can lead to the same kinds of issues that SRP aims to avoid in the first place. Striking the right balance in service boundaries requires a deep understanding of the domain and careful planning. This is where concepts like domain-driven design (DDD) can be helpful, as they provide a framework for identifying business capabilities and structuring services around them. DDD encourages teams to focus on the core business logic and to align services with business domains, which often leads to more manageable and focused microservices.

Another challenge is managing the communication between microservices, especially as the number of services increases. When each microservice has its own responsibility, it inevitably leads to a system where services must communicate with one another to perform more complex tasks. For instance, a service responsible for managing orders may need to communicate with services handling inventory, payments, and shipping. The communication between these services must be well-designed to avoid creating tight dependencies between them, which can undermine the benefits of SRP. Effective use of asynchronous messaging, service discovery, and API gateways can help manage service interactions without violating the independence of each service. It is essential to ensure that each service remains decoupled from the others as much as possible, allowing them to evolve independently without being affected by changes in other services.

Another aspect of SRP in microservices is the management of data. Each service typically manages its own data store, which aligns with the idea of encapsulating responsibility within a single service. However, managing data consistency across multiple services can be complex. In a monolithic system, data consistency is usually maintained through a single, central database, but in a microservices environment, each service might use a different type of database or storage mechanism. Techniques such as eventual consistency, event sourcing, and the Saga pattern can help manage data consistency across distributed services. However, these techniques also require careful design and understanding of the business processes, as they can introduce complexities related to transaction management, error handling, and data reconciliation.

Security is another critical consideration when designing microservices with SRP. Each service needs to ensure that it is secure and that only authorized users or systems can interact with it. This can be achieved by implementing security at the service level, using authentication and authorization mechanisms such as OAuth, JWT, or API keys. Additionally, secure communication protocols such as HTTPS should be employed to protect data in transit. By securing each service independently, microservices systems can minimize the risk of a single point of failure or a widespread security breach, which is often a concern in monolithic systems where a breach in one area can compromise the entire application.

The Single Responsibility Principle is a guiding force in the design of microservices, ensuring that each service has a clear and focused responsibility. By adhering to SRP, organizations can create microservices systems that are more maintainable, scalable, and resilient. SRP helps break down complex applications into manageable services that can evolve independently, making it easier to implement continuous delivery and to scale the system based on business needs. While challenges related to service boundaries, communication, and data consistency exist, the benefits of adhering to SRP far outweigh the complexities. By carefully considering the responsibilities of each service and using the right tools and strategies to manage dependencies, organizations can create a robust microservices architecture that delivers long-term value.

Communication Between Microservices: Synchronous vs. Asynchronous

Effective communication between microservices is a cornerstone of successful microservices architectures. Microservices are designed to be independently deployable and loosely coupled, and communication between them is essential to allow them to function as a cohesive system. However, when it comes to communication between services, there are two primary models to consider: synchronous and asynchronous. These communication models differ in terms of how services interact, the speed of interaction, and their overall impact on system performance, scalability, and fault tolerance. Understanding the differences between synchronous and asynchronous communication and how to leverage each model appropriately is crucial for building a robust microservices system.

Synchronous communication occurs when one service sends a request to another and waits for a response before proceeding. This model is similar to traditional client-server communication, where a client sends a request and the server processes the request and returns a response. In microservices, synchronous communication is typically achieved using protocols like HTTP or gRPC. The calling service makes a direct request to the target service and expects an immediate response. This type of communication is often used when the requesting service needs real-time data or when the interaction requires an immediate decision based on the response.

One of the advantages of synchronous communication is that it provides a straightforward way for services to exchange information. The request-response model is easy to understand and implement, making it an attractive choice for many use cases. Additionally, synchronous communication ensures that the calling service has the latest information from the target service, as it waits for the response before proceeding with any further operations. This makes synchronous communication a good choice when consistency and immediacy are critical, such as in scenarios where a service needs to perform a transaction or update a user profile in real-time.

However, there are several downsides to synchronous communication in microservices. One of the primary concerns is that it introduces tight coupling between services. Since a service must wait for a response before proceeding, any delays or failures in the target service can lead to increased latency or even complete failure of the calling service. This can be particularly problematic in large-scale systems with many interconnected services, where even small delays in one service can propagate through the system and affect overall performance. Furthermore, synchronous communication can create bottlenecks, as services become dependent on each other to complete requests in real-time. If the target service is under heavy load or unavailable, the entire chain of requests may be blocked, leading to degraded performance or downtime.

To mitigate these risks, it is essential to implement fault tolerance mechanisms in synchronous communication. Techniques such as timeouts, retries, and circuit breakers can help ensure that the system can recover from temporary failures and continue functioning smoothly. Additionally, load balancing and horizontal scaling can be used to distribute traffic more evenly across services and prevent any one service from becoming overwhelmed. Even with these safeguards in place, synchronous communication should be used selectively and only when it is essential for the system's functionality.

On the other hand, asynchronous communication involves services exchanging messages or events without waiting for an immediate response. In an asynchronous system, one service sends a request to another, but instead of waiting for a response, it continues with its own work. The receiving service processes the request in the background and, depending on the use case, may send a response or take action at a later time. Asynchronous communication is often implemented using message queues, event streaming platforms, or pub/sub systems, such as Apache Kafka or RabbitMQ.

The key advantage of asynchronous communication is that it decouples services, allowing them to operate independently. Since the calling service does not wait for a response, it can continue with other tasks, improving overall system performance and throughput. Asynchronous communication is particularly useful when services are performing background processing, such as processing payments, generating reports, or sending notifications. In these cases, the calling service does not need to wait for the processing to complete before moving on to other tasks. Instead, it can rely on eventual consistency, where the system eventually reaches a consistent state, even if the data or process is not immediately up to date.

Another benefit of asynchronous communication is that it can improve the fault tolerance and resiliency of the system. Since services are not dependent on one another to complete requests, the failure of one service does not immediately affect the others. If a service fails to process an event or message, it can retry the operation later, and the system can continue to function as normal. This makes asynchronous communication particularly useful in systems where reliability is critical, as it allows for delayed or retries of operations without blocking the entire system.

However, while asynchronous communication offers several advantages, it also introduces some challenges. One of the main challenges is managing the complexity of message processing. Since the calling service does not wait for an immediate response, it becomes more difficult to track the state of the system and ensure that all messages are processed correctly. This can lead to issues with message duplication, ordering, and consistency. For example, if a message is sent multiple times or processed out of order, it could lead to incorrect data or inconsistent state across services. To address these challenges, systems often rely on techniques such as idempotency, where operations can be repeated without causing unintended side effects, or event sourcing, where changes to the system state are captured as a series of events that can be replayed to restore consistency.

Another challenge with asynchronous communication is ensuring that the system remains responsive and does not become overwhelmed by a backlog of unprocessed messages. To mitigate this, it is essential to implement proper message queue management and ensure that messages are processed in a timely manner. Message brokers typically provide features such as message prioritization, dead-letter queues, and flow control to help manage the flow of messages and prevent congestion.

Choosing between synchronous and asynchronous communication is not always a straightforward decision. In many cases, a hybrid approach is used, where both synchronous and asynchronous communication are employed based on the specific requirements of the system. For example, a system might use synchronous communication for real-time interactions, such as retrieving user information, and asynchronous communication for background tasks, such as processing orders or sending notifications. This approach allows the system to take advantage of the strengths of both models while minimizing the drawbacks of each.

When designing communication strategies for microservices, it is important to carefully consider the needs of the application and the trade-offs between synchronous and asynchronous communication.

Synchronous communication is well-suited for scenarios where real-time data and immediate responses are required, but it comes with risks related to tight coupling, latency, and bottlenecks. Asynchronous communication, on the other hand, offers greater flexibility, scalability, and fault tolerance, but it introduces challenges related to message processing and eventual consistency. By understanding the strengths and weaknesses of both communication models, developers can design microservices systems that are both efficient and resilient, capable of handling a wide range of workloads and use cases.

Choosing the Right Database for Microservices

Choosing the right database for microservices is a critical decision that impacts the overall performance, scalability, and maintainability of the system. In a microservices architecture, each service is designed to be independent, with its own responsibility and often its own database. This design principle, known as database per service, ensures that services remain decoupled, allowing them to evolve independently and scale according to specific needs. However, this approach introduces challenges when it comes to choosing the most suitable database technology for each service. The database choice must align with the unique requirements of the service, including its data access patterns, consistency needs, and performance expectations.

One of the key considerations in selecting a database for microservices is the nature of the data that the service will handle. Microservices are designed to handle different aspects of an application, and each service may need to manage different types of data. Some services may require relational data, while others may need to handle unstructured or semi-structured data. Relational databases like MySQL, PostgreSQL, and SQL Server are well-suited for applications that require structured data and strong consistency guarantees, such as transactional systems that need to ensure data integrity. On the other hand, NoSQL databases like MongoDB, Cassandra, and Couchbase are more appropriate for applications that require scalability, high availability, and flexibility in handling unstructured data. These NoSQL databases are often used when dealing with large amounts of data, frequent schema changes, or when the service needs to handle high-throughput operations.

The consistency model required by the service is another important factor when selecting a database. In a microservices environment, each service typically has its own database, which means that maintaining consistency across services can be challenging. Relational databases enforce strong consistency using ACID (Atomicity, Consistency, Isolation, Durability) properties, which ensure that transactions are processed reliably. However, in a distributed system with multiple microservices, maintaining ACID properties across services can lead to performance bottlenecks and reduced scalability. For many microservices architectures, particularly those designed to scale horizontally, a more relaxed consistency model may be appropriate. NoSQL databases often support eventual consistency, where the system guarantees that data will eventually reach a consistent state, but there may be temporary inconsistencies between services. This trade-off between consistency and availability is known as the CAP theorem, and understanding the needs of the application will help determine which database technology is the most suitable.

Another factor to consider when choosing a database is the service's performance requirements. Different databases excel at different types of workloads, so understanding the specific data access patterns and usage scenarios is crucial. For example, a service that performs complex queries with many joins and transactions might benefit from a relational database, as it is designed to handle these types of operations efficiently. In contrast, a service that requires fast writes and low-latency reads, such as a real-time analytics service or a recommendation engine, might be better served by a NoSQL database optimized for high-throughput operations. For services that need to handle a high volume of data across multiple nodes, distributed databases like Cassandra or Amazon DynamoDB provide excellent scalability and fault tolerance. These databases are designed to distribute data across a large number of servers, ensuring that the service can handle growing amounts of data without sacrificing performance.

Scalability is one of the defining characteristics of microservices, and the database choice plays a significant role in supporting that scalability. Microservices are often deployed in a cloud-native environment, where services are dynamically scaled up or down to handle varying loads. The database must be able to scale independently to accommodate changes in the demand for the service. Relational databases traditionally scale vertically, meaning that they require more powerful hardware or more resources on a single server to handle increased load. While vertical scaling can work for smaller systems, it becomes expensive and less efficient as the system grows. NoSQL databases, on the other hand, typically scale horizontally by distributing data across multiple nodes, allowing them to handle much larger volumes of data and higher levels of traffic. This horizontal scalability is essential for microservices that need to handle large amounts of data or traffic without affecting performance.

Another aspect of database selection for microservices is the need for data isolation and autonomy between services. Each microservice is intended to be an independent unit of functionality, and part of this independence includes managing its own database. This approach allows services to evolve without being constrained by the database schema of other services. However, when multiple services require access to shared data, maintaining data consistency and ensuring smooth communication between databases can become complex. Some microservices architectures may use event-driven patterns, such as event sourcing or CQRS (Command Query Responsibility Segregation), to handle communication between services without requiring direct database access. These patterns help ensure that services remain decoupled while still being able to share data asynchronously. For example, in an event-driven architecture, one service can emit an event that other services listen to, allowing them to update their own databases accordingly. This pattern helps maintain autonomy between services while still enabling data synchronization.

Data replication and availability are additional considerations when choosing a database for microservices. Microservices typically run in distributed environments where services are deployed across multiple nodes or even multiple geographic regions. To ensure that data is always available, even in the event of server or network failures, databases must support replication. Many modern databases, both relational and NoSQL, offer built-in replication features that allow data to be copied across multiple nodes or data centers. This ensures that even if one node becomes unavailable, the data can still be accessed from another node. Additionally, replication helps improve read performance by distributing the read workload across multiple instances of the database. However, replication introduces challenges related to data consistency and conflict resolution, particularly when services update data concurrently. Understanding the trade-offs between availability and consistency is essential when selecting a database for microservices, as it will influence the system's overall reliability and fault tolerance.

The operational overhead of managing databases is another factor to consider in the database selection process. While relational databases and NoSQL databases both offer powerful features, they also come with operational complexities. Managing and maintaining databases, including handling backups, updates, scaling, and security, can be time-consuming and error-prone, especially in a distributed environment with multiple microservices. Some organizations may opt for managed database services, such as Amazon RDS, Google Cloud SQL, or MongoDB Atlas, to offload much of the operational burden. These managed services provide automatic backups, monitoring, scaling, and patching, allowing development teams to focus on building and improving the application rather than managing the database infrastructure. For organizations with limited database expertise or those looking to streamline operations, using managed database services can reduce the complexity and operational overhead of maintaining multiple databases.

Choosing the right database for microservices requires a deep understanding of the specific needs of each service and the overall system. The database should align with the data model, consistency requirements, scalability goals, and performance expectations of the service it supports. In many cases, a polyglot persistence approach—where different databases are used for different services—may be the most appropriate solution. By selecting the right database technology for each microservice, organizations can ensure that their systems are both scalable and maintainable, capable of handling large volumes of data while supporting independent, loosely coupled services. The right database choice can significantly impact the overall success of a microservices architecture, making it a crucial decision in the design process.

Event-Driven Architectures in Microservices

Event-driven architectures (EDA) have become an essential pattern in microservices design due to their ability to decouple services and facilitate asynchronous communication between them. In an event-driven system, microservices do not directly call one another via synchronous APIs; instead, they emit events and listen for events. This paradigm shifts the system from a request-response model to one based on the publication and consumption of events. Events, in this context, represent significant state changes or occurrences within the system that other services may need to respond to. Event-driven architectures enable microservices to operate more autonomously, scale efficiently, and respond dynamically to system-wide changes. This approach is particularly valuable in systems that require high scalability, resilience, and flexibility.

In an event-driven architecture, services are often designed to act as event producers and event consumers. When an event occurs, a service publishes that event to a messaging system, which acts as an intermediary. Other services that are interested in this event can then subscribe to it and take appropriate actions when the event is received. The event itself typically contains information about the state change or action that has occurred, such as an order being placed or a payment being processed. By relying on events, services can remain loosely coupled, as they do not need to directly communicate with each other to share data or trigger actions. This loose coupling is one of the key benefits of event-driven architectures, as it allows services to evolve independently, scale separately, and function without being tightly integrated.

A critical feature of event-driven architectures is the use of an event bus or a message broker. The event bus acts as the central point of communication, enabling the decoupling of producers and consumers of events. Messaging systems like Apache Kafka, RabbitMQ, and Amazon SNS are commonly used as the event bus in microservices architectures. These systems handle the distribution of events to the appropriate services, ensuring that they are reliably delivered even in distributed, fault-tolerant systems. One of the primary advantages of using an event bus is that it enables asynchronous communication between services, which reduces the latency of requests and ensures that services do not block each other while waiting for responses. The event-driven model also improves system resiliency, as services can continue to operate even if other services are temporarily unavailable. When a service becomes available again, it can simply catch up on the events it missed.

Event-driven architectures are especially well-suited for systems that need to handle high throughput or frequent changes in state. For example, an e-commerce system might have services for inventory management, order processing, and shipping, each of which can be loosely coupled by emitting and subscribing to events. When a customer places an order, the order service can emit an event that triggers the inventory service to update the stock levels. Similarly, the shipping service can listen for events related to order fulfillment and handle logistics tasks when an order is ready to ship. The benefits of this approach become particularly apparent as the number of services in the system grows. Instead of managing direct API calls between every service, event-driven communication reduces the number of dependencies and simplifies system architecture.

One of the significant advantages of event-driven microservices is their ability to improve system scalability. Since services communicate asynchronously through events, they can scale independently based on demand. For example, if a service is handling a high volume of events, it can be scaled up to accommodate the increased load without impacting other services. This granular approach to scaling is more efficient than scaling an entire monolithic application or even a set of tightly coupled services. In addition, the event bus allows for easy load balancing, as events can be distributed across multiple instances of a service to ensure optimal resource utilization.

Despite these advantages, event-driven architectures introduce new challenges that need to be addressed to ensure their effectiveness. One of the primary challenges is managing the ordering and consistency of events. In a distributed system, events may not always be processed in the order they are emitted, which can lead to inconsistencies or unexpected behavior. For example, if an event related to updating a customer's address is processed before an event related to updating their order, it may result in outdated or incorrect data. Techniques such as event versioning, idempotent event processing, and careful event sequencing can help manage these issues. Event versioning involves creating new versions of events when the structure or meaning of an event changes, while idempotent event processing ensures that the same event can be processed multiple times without causing issues.

Another challenge in event-driven architectures is ensuring that events are reliably delivered to all interested consumers. Messaging systems typically provide mechanisms for ensuring that events are not lost, but these systems are not infallible. In cases where an event fails to be delivered or processed, it is essential to have mechanisms in place to handle retries and dead-letter queues, which store undeliverable messages for later inspection. Dead-letter queues are particularly useful for diagnosing issues and ensuring that critical events are not lost in the system. Moreover, systems must be designed to handle potential message duplication, ensuring that repeated processing of the same event does not lead to inconsistent or erroneous outcomes.

Event-driven architectures also rely heavily on eventual consistency, as opposed to the strong consistency often found in traditional relational databases. In an event-driven system, services may not always have the most up-to-date view of the data, as they process events asynchronously. This can lead to temporary inconsistencies between services, which can be acceptable in many scenarios but needs to be carefully managed. Eventual consistency is the concept that, over time, all services will converge on the same state, but there may be periods where services have slightly out-of-date data. Techniques such as event sourcing and the use of distributed transactions can help ensure that eventual consistency is achieved while maintaining the integrity of the system.

Event-driven architectures are also highly effective in enabling real-time processing. For instance, a service might be responsible for processing high-velocity events such as user activity tracking, sensor data collection, or financial transactions. These services can consume and process events in real-time, enabling immediate responses to changes in the system. Real-time event processing frameworks, such as Apache Flink or Apache Storm, can be integrated into microservices to allow for sophisticated event processing capabilities like complex event detection, aggregation, and analytics. By processing events as they occur, event-driven architectures allow for faster decision-making and enable systems to respond to changes immediately, providing a competitive advantage in industries that require real-time data processing.

As microservices systems evolve, event-driven architectures become more complex, and managing them becomes a key challenge. Event-driven systems often result in highly distributed, loosely coupled services, which makes monitoring and debugging more difficult. Tracking events as they flow through different services requires sophisticated logging, tracing, and monitoring tools. Distributed tracing solutions like Zipkin, Jaeger, and OpenTelemetry help developers track the journey of events across services, making it easier to diagnose issues and understand system behavior. These tools are essential for maintaining visibility in a complex, event-driven environment, allowing for proactive management and continuous optimization.

Event-driven architectures provide a powerful way to design microservices systems that are flexible, scalable, and resilient. By decoupling services through asynchronous communication, they enable greater autonomy and responsiveness while improving system scalability and fault tolerance. However, event-driven systems come with challenges related to event ordering, consistency, and reliable delivery. These challenges require careful consideration and the implementation of techniques to ensure the smooth operation of the system. When designed and managed correctly, event-driven architectures can transform how microservices systems interact, enabling real-time processing, better scalability, and more robust fault tolerance.

Microservices Security Best Practices

In a microservices architecture, security becomes more complex than in traditional monolithic systems due to the distributed nature of the services and their communication. Each microservice in the architecture typically has its own responsibilities and interacts with other services, often over a network. This distributed setup introduces various security concerns such as unauthorized access, data breaches, and service vulnerabilities. Ensuring the security of a microservices-based system requires a holistic approach that addresses both the individual services and their interactions. Adhering to security best practices is essential to safeguard against potential threats, reduce vulnerabilities, and maintain the integrity of the system.

One of the fundamental security practices for microservices is ensuring strong authentication and authorization mechanisms. Since microservices are designed to operate independently, each service needs to verify the identity of the clients or other services that are requesting access. Implementing secure authentication methods, such as OAuth 2.0 or JSON Web Tokens (JWT), helps ensure that only authorized entities can access the services. OAuth 2.0, for instance, is widely used for token-based authentication, where a client obtains an access token after providing valid credentials. This token is then used to authenticate subsequent requests to other services. Using JWTs as the token format ensures that the identity and permissions of the user or service are securely transmitted between services, reducing the risk of identity theft or unauthorized access.

Authorization goes hand in hand with authentication, ensuring that authenticated entities have the appropriate permissions to access resources. In microservices, implementing role-based access control (RBAC) or attribute-based access control (ABAC) can help ensure that users or services are granted the least privilege necessary to perform their tasks. Each microservice can enforce its own set of access policies, and access decisions can be based on the roles or attributes of the requesting entity. This decentralized approach to authorization allows microservices to operate independently while maintaining tight control over access to sensitive data and resources.

Another important security practice is the use of encryption for data in transit and at rest. Since microservices typically communicate over a network, data must be encrypted to protect it from interception by malicious actors. Using secure communication protocols, such as HTTPS (SSL/TLS), ensures that data transmitted between services remains private and cannot be tampered with. Encryption should also be applied to sensitive data stored within each microservice's database to prevent unauthorized access in the event of a data breach. Strong encryption algorithms and key management practices must be employed to protect both data in transit and at rest, reducing the likelihood of data leaks or breaches.

Service-to-service communication poses another challenge in securing a microservices architecture. Since services often need to interact with each other, it is crucial to establish secure communication channels. Mutual TLS (Transport Layer Security) is a common approach for securing service-to-service communication. With mutual TLS, both the client and the server authenticate each other using certificates, ensuring that only trusted services can communicate with each other. This approach not only provides encryption but also authenticates both the service making the request and the service receiving it, reducing the risk of man-in-the-middle attacks or unauthorized access between services.

Securing the microservices ecosystem requires a robust API management strategy. As APIs are the primary means by which microservices communicate, they become a potential attack vector if not properly secured. Implementing API gateways can help centralize security policies, such as authentication, rate limiting, and logging, for all services. An API gateway can act as a gatekeeper, validating incoming requests before they reach individual services. Additionally, the API gateway can enforce security policies such as filtering out malicious requests, monitoring for unusual activity, and ensuring that only authorized requests are allowed through to the underlying services. By centralizing security at the gateway, microservices can focus on their core business logic, while security concerns are managed more efficiently.

Another crucial aspect of microservices security is the implementation of logging and monitoring for proactive threat detection. In a distributed system, monitoring the health and behavior of each service is critical for identifying potential security threats early. Centralized logging solutions, such as ELK stack (Elasticsearch, Logstash, and Kibana) or Fluentd, aggregate logs from various services, providing a unified view of the system's activity. These logs can be analyzed for unusual patterns that may indicate security incidents, such as failed authentication attempts or unexpected traffic spikes. Implementing monitoring tools that track the performance and security of the system, such as Prometheus and Grafana, enables teams to detect anomalies and respond quickly to any potential breaches.

Another critical best practice in microservices security is the principle of "zero trust." In a zero-trust model, security is not assumed based on network boundaries or the traditional perimeter. Instead, every request, whether it comes from inside or outside the system, is treated as potentially malicious. This means that every service must authenticate and authorize every request before it is allowed to interact with any other service, even if the request comes from a trusted internal service. The zero-trust approach helps ensure that no single service is trusted implicitly and that security measures are enforced at every layer of the system.

Additionally, securing microservices involves minimizing the attack surface. Each microservice should follow the principle of least privilege, meaning that it should only have access to the resources and data necessary for its specific function. By limiting the scope of each service's responsibilities, the potential damage caused by a security breach is minimized. This principle applies not only to the services themselves but also to the databases they interact with. Each service should have its own isolated database, ensuring that an attack on one service does not compromise the data of other services. Furthermore, microservices should be isolated in terms of network access, with firewalls and network segmentation to prevent unauthorized access between services.

Implementing secure software development practices is another important consideration in the security of microservices. Regular code reviews, static code analysis, and automated security testing can help identify vulnerabilities early in the development process. Practices such as secure coding guidelines, dependency management, and patching known vulnerabilities also play a vital role in maintaining the security of the system. Integrating security into the development lifecycle through DevSecOps practices ensures that security is considered at every stage, from design and development to deployment and maintenance.

Finally, ensuring the security of microservices requires regular audits and vulnerability assessments. As the microservices architecture evolves, new vulnerabilities can emerge, and existing ones can be exploited. Regular penetration testing, vulnerability scanning, and security audits can help identify potential risks and ensure that security measures are up to date. Implementing a continuous improvement process for security practices ensures that the system remains resilient against emerging threats and adapts to new security challenges.

Securing microservices requires a multi-faceted approach that spans authentication, authorization, encryption, secure communication, and monitoring. By following these security best practices, organizations can build robust, resilient microservices architectures that minimize the risk of data breaches, unauthorized access, and system vulnerabilities. Ensuring the security of microservices is an ongoing effort, requiring constant vigilance, adaptation, and the integration of security throughout the development and operational lifecycle. With the right security measures in place, organizations can confidently deploy and scale microservices systems without compromising the integrity of their data or services.

Service Discovery in Microservices Architectures

In a microservices architecture, service discovery is a critical component that enables services to dynamically locate and communicate with each other in a distributed environment. Microservices are designed to be independently deployable, and as a result, the locations of individual services may change frequently, particularly in cloud-native or containerized environments. Traditional static configurations where services communicate using hardcoded IP addresses or fixed endpoints do not scale well in such dynamic systems. Service discovery addresses this challenge by allowing microservices to automatically discover and connect to each other, regardless of where they are deployed or how their locations may change over time. This mechanism is essential for maintaining the fluid, flexible nature of microservices while ensuring reliable communication and optimal system performance.

In essence, service discovery is the process by which a service can find other services that it needs to communicate with, without requiring manual configuration. In a typical microservices system, a service may need to communicate with several other services to fulfill a user request or perform a business function. For example, an order service might need to query the inventory service to check product availability or interact with a payment service to process a transaction. Without service discovery, the order service would need to know the exact location of the inventory and payment services, which is not feasible in a dynamic environment where services can scale up or down and where instances of a service may be created or destroyed at any given time.

Service discovery can be broken down into two major components: service registration and service lookup. Service registration involves the process by which a service makes itself discoverable by other services. When a service instance is deployed, it registers its location (typically an IP address and port) with a service registry, which acts as a central directory that stores the current locations of all available services. Service lookup, on the other hand, refers to the process by which a service queries the service registry to find the location of another service it needs to communicate with. The registry provides the service instance with the most up-to-date information about where to reach the other services, thereby eliminating the need for hardcoded configurations.

There are two main types of service discovery: client-side and server-side. In client-side service discovery, the client (i.e., the calling service) is responsible for querying the service registry to find the appropriate instance of a service. Once the client has the service's location, it can directly send requests to the service instance. The client also typically handles load balancing by distributing requests to multiple instances of a service, ensuring optimal resource utilization. One of the advantages of client-side service discovery is that it allows for flexibility and decentralization, as each service is responsible for finding and managing the services it depends on. However, this can also add complexity to the client, as it needs to handle both service discovery and load balancing logic.

Server-side service discovery, on the other hand, shifts the responsibility for service discovery to a dedicated component, often a load balancer or an API gateway. In this model, when a service needs to call another service, it sends its request to the load balancer or API gateway, which is responsible for querying the service registry, selecting an appropriate service instance, and forwarding the request to that instance. Server-side discovery simplifies the client's responsibilities, as it does not need to worry about service discovery or load balancing. It is also easier to manage, as the service discovery logic is centralized. However, this approach introduces a potential single point of failure, as the load balancer or API gateway becomes an essential component for service communication. Ensuring high availability and fault tolerance of these components is therefore critical.

Service discovery typically relies on a service registry, which is a centralized database that keeps track of the available services and their current locations. There are several popular tools and frameworks for implementing service registries in microservices architectures. Consul, Zookeeper, and Eureka are some of the most commonly used service registries. These tools provide APIs for registering and discovering services, as well as features for health checks, which allow services to periodically report their availability to the registry. If a service instance becomes unhealthy or fails, the service registry can remove it from the list of available instances, ensuring that requests are not sent to unavailable services. This mechanism helps maintain the reliability and resilience of the system by preventing failed services from being used in communication.

In addition to providing service registration and discovery, these tools often include features for monitoring and maintaining the health of services. Health checks are an important part of service discovery, as they ensure that services are functioning correctly and are able to handle requests. For example, a service can periodically check its own health and report this status to the service registry, which can then make the service unavailable if it is not responding correctly. By incorporating health checks into the service discovery process, microservices architectures can become more resilient, as they can automatically adjust to failures by redirecting traffic away from unhealthy services.

One of the key benefits of service discovery in microservices architectures is its ability to support dynamic scaling. Microservices often operate in environments like Kubernetes or cloud platforms, where services can scale in and out based on traffic patterns or resource utilization. As services are scaled up, new instances of the service are automatically registered with the service registry, making them discoverable to other services. Conversely, when services are scaled down, their instances are unregistered from the registry, preventing requests from being sent to them. This automatic scaling and registration process ensures that the system can handle changes in load without manual intervention, allowing for efficient resource utilization and optimal performance.

However, service discovery introduces certain challenges, particularly in highly dynamic and distributed environments. One challenge is managing the performance of the service registry itself. As the number of services in the system grows, the service registry can become a bottleneck, particularly if it is not designed to handle high volumes of requests. It is crucial to ensure that the service registry is highly available and scalable, as any downtime or failure of the registry can disrupt the entire communication process between services. To mitigate this risk, many organizations implement redundant and distributed service registries to ensure that the system can continue functioning even if one instance of the registry fails.

Another challenge with service discovery is ensuring secure communication between services. Since services are often communicating over a network, securing service discovery traffic is essential to prevent unauthorized access and ensure data integrity. Service discovery solutions often integrate with authentication and authorization mechanisms, such as mutual TLS (Transport Layer Security), to encrypt communication between services and authenticate service identities. This helps ensure that only authorized services can register with the service registry and discover other services, mitigating the risk of man-in-the-middle attacks or unauthorized access.

The integration of service discovery with modern orchestration platforms like Kubernetes has made the management of microservices much easier. Kubernetes includes built-in service discovery capabilities that automatically register services and provide DNS-based resolution for service locations. This integration simplifies the implementation of service discovery by automating many of the processes involved, such as service registration, load balancing, and scaling. As a result, developers can focus more on the functionality of their services rather than the complexities of service discovery and management.

Service discovery is a vital component of microservices architectures, enabling services to dynamically locate and communicate with each other in distributed systems. By automating the discovery process and using a service registry, microservices can scale, adapt, and maintain high levels of performance and availability. While service discovery introduces certain challenges related to scalability, security, and registry performance, the benefits far outweigh these challenges, providing organizations with the flexibility and agility needed to build and manage complex, distributed systems.

API Gateways and Their Role in Microservices

In a microservices architecture, services are typically designed to be independent, small, and loosely coupled, each responsible for a specific business function. While this independence offers flexibility and scalability, it also introduces challenges when it comes to managing communication between services. Each microservice may expose its own API, leading to a complex network of endpoints that must be accessed by clients or other services. This is where API gateways come into play. An API gateway acts as a reverse proxy that sits between clients and microservices, handling requests, routing them to the appropriate service, and performing various cross-cutting tasks such as authentication, load balancing, rate limiting, and response aggregation. The use of an API gateway simplifies the interaction between clients and microservices, centralizing the management of requests and improving the overall efficiency and maintainability of the system.

One of the primary roles of an API gateway is to provide a single entry point for all client requests to the microservices ecosystem. In a traditional monolithic system, clients interact directly with the application's components through a unified API. In microservices, however, clients must interact with multiple independent services, each with its own API. Without an API gateway, this would require clients to manage communication with several services, potentially resulting in inefficient and fragmented communication. The API gateway abstracts this complexity by consolidating all service interactions into a single endpoint. Clients send requests to the gateway, which then routes those requests to the appropriate microservice based on the request's path, headers, or other routing rules. This centralization simplifies client-side logic, as clients no longer need to manage the complexities of interacting with multiple services.

API gateways also serve as a mediator for handling cross-cutting concerns that are common to multiple microservices. One such concern is authentication and authorization. In a microservices environment, each service may have its own security policies, and managing authentication across numerous endpoints can become cumbersome. The API gateway can centralize authentication, ensuring that every incoming request is validated before it reaches any service. This is typically done using standards like OAuth 2.0 or JWT, which allow the API gateway to authenticate users or services based on tokens. Once a request is authenticated, the gateway can also enforce authorization policies, ensuring that users or services have the appropriate permissions to access the requested resource. By centralizing security at the gateway, the system ensures that individual services are not burdened with security responsibilities, allowing them to focus on business logic.

Another key function of the API gateway is load balancing. In a microservices system, individual services are often deployed in multiple instances to handle varying levels of traffic and ensure high availability. The API gateway can manage load balancing by distributing incoming requests across multiple instances of a service. This ensures that no single instance is overwhelmed with traffic and helps optimize resource utilization. Load balancing can be based on various algorithms, such as round-robin, least connections, or weighted distribution, depending on the specific needs of the system. By handling load balancing centrally, the API gateway eliminates the need for each service to manage its own load balancing logic, reducing complexity and improving system efficiency.

Rate limiting is another important feature that can be implemented at the API gateway level. In a microservices architecture, certain services may be more sensitive to high traffic loads than others. The API gateway can enforce rate limits to prevent overloading particular services and ensure that the system remains responsive under heavy traffic conditions. For example, the API gateway can limit the number of requests a client or user can make within a specific time period, preventing abuse or unintentional overload. Rate limiting can also be used to protect against denial-of-service (DoS) attacks, where an attacker floods the system with a large number of requests. By handling rate limiting at the gateway level, the system can prevent malicious actors from targeting individual services and ensure that the overall system remains secure and performant.

API gateways can also play a crucial role in response aggregation. In a microservices architecture, a single client request may require data from multiple services. Without an API gateway, the client would need to send multiple requests to different services and then combine the responses, which can introduce unnecessary complexity and latency. The API gateway can aggregate responses from multiple services into a single response, reducing the number of round trips the client needs to make and simplifying the client's logic. This is particularly useful in scenarios where a client needs to retrieve related data from different services, such as displaying a user's profile, which may involve retrieving information from both a user service and a profile service. By aggregating responses at the gateway, the system can streamline communication and improve overall performance.

In addition to these operational features, an API gateway can also enhance observability in a microservices architecture. With many independent services communicating with one another, it can be challenging to track the flow of requests and identify performance bottlenecks or failures. The API gateway can collect logs, metrics, and traces for all incoming and outgoing requests, providing a centralized view of system activity. This enables developers and operators to monitor traffic patterns, identify slow or failing services, and quickly diagnose issues. By centralizing observability at the gateway, the system makes it easier to track and troubleshoot issues, improving overall reliability and maintainability.

While API gateways provide numerous benefits, they also introduce certain challenges. One of the main concerns is the potential for the gateway to become a single point of failure. Since the gateway serves as the central entry point for all client requests, any failure in the gateway can disrupt the entire system. To mitigate this risk, it is essential to ensure that the API gateway is highly available and fault-tolerant. This can be achieved through techniques such as load balancing across multiple gateway instances, implementing health checks, and using failover mechanisms. Additionally, the gateway should be designed to handle traffic spikes and be able to scale horizontally to meet increased demand.

Another challenge is the increased latency introduced by the API gateway. Since all requests must pass through the gateway before reaching the microservices, there is a risk of adding additional processing time to each request. To minimize this latency, it is important to optimize the gateway's performance and ensure that it can handle high throughput with minimal overhead. Caching is one technique that can help reduce latency by storing frequently requested data at the gateway, reducing the need to make repeated requests to the underlying services.

API gateways also need to be carefully managed to ensure they do not become a bottleneck in the system. As the number of microservices increases, the complexity of the API gateway grows, and it becomes essential to ensure that the gateway is well-maintained and properly configured. Poorly designed or misconfigured API gateways can create performance issues and disrupt the efficient functioning of the entire microservices system.

API gateways play a central role in the management of communication between clients and microservices, providing a range of important features such as routing, authentication, load balancing, rate limiting, response aggregation, and observability. By centralizing these cross-cutting concerns, API gateways simplify the architecture, improve security, and streamline the interaction between services. Despite the potential challenges, such as the risk of single points of failure and increased latency, the use of an API gateway is essential for ensuring the smooth operation of microservices systems at scale. The API gateway enables developers to focus on building and maintaining microservices while the gateway manages the complexities of service-to-client communication and service intercommunication.

Managing Service Dependencies in Microservices

In microservices architectures, one of the most significant challenges is managing the dependencies between services. Unlike monolithic applications, where all components reside in the same codebase and can easily communicate through direct function calls or shared resources, microservices are distributed and independent. Each service is a standalone unit with its own database, logic, and resources, but they often need to interact with one another to complete a business transaction or fulfill a user request. Managing these interdependencies while maintaining the flexibility, scalability, and fault tolerance that microservices promise is crucial for the success of a microservices-based system.

When designing microservices, the first step is to understand that dependencies are inevitable. Microservices rarely operate in isolation; instead, they collaborate with one another through well-defined APIs or messaging systems. This inter-service communication can involve various complexities, such as data consistency, transactional integrity, or managing distributed state. One of the primary concerns when managing service dependencies is ensuring that the communication between services is reliable, efficient, and secure. Without proper management, these dependencies can lead to tight coupling, which undermines the independence and scalability that microservices are designed to provide.

To manage service dependencies effectively, it is essential to minimize the tight coupling between services. Tight coupling occurs when services rely too heavily on each other, such that changes to one service require changes to others. This situation makes it difficult to scale, maintain, and evolve services independently. Microservices should ideally follow the principle of loose coupling, meaning that they communicate with one another without being directly dependent on the internal implementation of other services. Instead of relying on direct communication between services, microservices should interact through APIs or event-driven architectures that abstract away the details of the other service's implementation. This decoupling allows each service to evolve independently, without causing disruptions in the rest of the system.

An essential technique for managing service dependencies is service orchestration. In microservices, orchestration refers to the management and coordination of interactions between services to ensure that they work together to achieve a business goal. This is typically handled by an orchestrator, which could be a central service or a set of services that manage the flow of data and operations between microservices. The orchestrator ensures that each service performs its part of the task and manages the dependencies between them. For example, in an e-commerce system, an order service might orchestrate the process of taking an order, checking inventory, calculating prices, processing payment, and initiating shipping. The orchestrator would coordinate the communication between the various services that perform these tasks, ensuring that they all work together seamlessly.

While orchestration is useful, it can introduce challenges such as a single point of failure and complexity in managing the flow of requests. To mitigate these risks, some organizations prefer to use choreography, where services communicate directly with one another without a central orchestrator. In a choreographed system, each service knows its role in a larger business process and can interact with other services based on events or messages. For example, a payment service might listen for events from the order service, such as when an order is placed, and then send a message to the inventory service to reserve stock. Choreography eliminates the need for a central orchestrator and allows services to remain autonomous, but it can be harder to manage as the number of services and dependencies grows.

Another key aspect of managing service dependencies is ensuring data consistency across services. In a monolithic system, data consistency is typically maintained through a single, centralized database. However, in microservices, each service often has its own database, leading to challenges in ensuring that data remains consistent across services. Traditional database transactions, which ensure consistency in monolithic systems, cannot be easily applied in a distributed environment. To address this issue, microservices architectures often rely on eventual consistency, where updates to data in one service are propagated to other services over time. While this approach allows services to function independently, it introduces the risk of temporary data inconsistencies. To manage eventual consistency, techniques such as event sourcing, CQRS (Command Query Responsibility Segregation), and the Saga pattern can be employed. These patterns help ensure that data is eventually synchronized across services, even if immediate consistency cannot be guaranteed.

Service dependencies also need to be managed in terms of fault tolerance. Since microservices are distributed systems, there is always the potential for failure. A failure in one service should not bring down the entire system, which means that service dependencies need to be resilient and fault-tolerant. One way to achieve this is by implementing retries, timeouts, and circuit breakers. A retry mechanism ensures that a failed request is retried a certain number of times before giving up, while a timeout ensures that a request does not hang indefinitely if a service is unavailable. Circuit breakers are particularly important in preventing cascading failures, where one service failure causes other services to fail. When a circuit breaker is triggered, it temporarily halts communication with the failing service and prevents further requests, allowing the system to recover. These mechanisms ensure that service dependencies are robust and that the overall system can continue functioning even in the face of failures.

Another important consideration is versioning and managing changes to service APIs. As microservices evolve, their APIs may change, introducing breaking changes that affect other services that depend on them. To prevent disruptions, it is essential to have a strategy for managing API versioning and ensuring backward compatibility. One approach is to implement versioning directly within the API, where new versions of the service API are introduced while still supporting older versions for a period of time. This allows dependent services to continue functioning while they are updated to work with the new version. Another approach is to use feature toggles or canary releases to gradually roll out new functionality, ensuring that only a subset of users or services are affected by changes until they are fully stable.

Service dependencies in microservices also need to be managed in terms of their communication patterns. Microservices often use different communication models, such as synchronous RESTful APIs or asynchronous messaging systems, to interact with one another. Synchronous communication can introduce latency and coupling between services, as each service must wait for a response before continuing. Asynchronous communication, on the other hand, allows services to operate independently, but it can be more difficult to manage, particularly when dealing with issues such as message duplication or ordering. Choosing the right communication model for each service dependency depends on factors such as the type of operation being performed, the level of consistency required, and the overall system architecture. By carefully managing communication patterns, microservices can ensure that they function efficiently and can scale to meet the needs of the business.

Finally, managing service dependencies in microservices requires effective monitoring and observability. With many services communicating with one another, it can be difficult to track the flow of requests and identify where issues are occurring. Centralized logging, distributed tracing, and metrics collection tools are essential for providing visibility into the system's behavior. Tools like Prometheus, Grafana, Zipkin, and ELK stack allow developers to monitor the performance of services, identify bottlenecks, and quickly diagnose issues. By ensuring that service dependencies are observable, teams can proactively address issues and optimize the performance of the system.

Managing service dependencies in microservices is a complex but essential task that requires careful design and planning. By minimizing tight coupling, implementing fault tolerance mechanisms, ensuring data consistency, managing API versioning, and selecting appropriate communication patterns, organizations can build microservices architectures that are scalable, resilient, and maintainable. Effective management of service dependencies enables microservices to work together seamlessly while maintaining their autonomy and flexibility.

Ensuring Fault Tolerance and Resilience in Microservices

In the world of microservices, ensuring fault tolerance and resilience is of paramount importance. A microservices architecture, by its very nature, is distributed and consists of many independent services that work together to fulfill business requirements. This distributed nature, while offering many advantages such as scalability and flexibility, also introduces complexity, particularly when it comes to handling failures. Since microservices communicate over a network, which is prone to latency and interruptions, systems must be designed to handle failures gracefully without causing widespread disruptions. Fault tolerance and resilience are critical in making sure that the system continues to function even in the face of partial failures, ensuring that users experience minimal impact and that the system remains reliable over time.

One of the primary goals when building resilient microservices is to design services that can operate independently of one another as much as possible. This decoupling of services helps mitigate the impact of a failure in any single service. In a traditional monolithic application, a failure in one component might bring down the entire system, but in a microservices environment, a failure in one service should ideally not affect others. To achieve this level of independence, microservices should be designed to handle failures locally. Each service should have the ability to fail gracefully, ensuring that its failure does not cascade and cause a chain reaction that could affect the entire system. For example, when a service fails, it should not block the entire system from processing other requests or performing other operations.

A critical technique to achieve fault tolerance is implementing retries. When a service makes a request to another service, there is always the possibility that the request will fail due to temporary issues, such as network congestion, timeouts, or brief service unavailability. In such cases, instead of failing immediately, the service can retry the request a predefined number of times before giving up. This retry mechanism should be configured with appropriate backoff strategies, such as exponential backoff, which gradually increases the wait time between retry attempts. This approach helps ensure that temporary issues are resolved without overwhelming the system with retries, while still allowing the system to recover from short-lived failures.

Timeouts also play a crucial role in fault tolerance. When a service makes a request to another service, it must be able to specify how long it is willing to wait for a response. If the service does not respond within the specified timeout period, the calling service should abandon the request and move on. Setting appropriate timeouts prevents services from waiting indefinitely for a response, which could block other operations and degrade the performance of the system. It is important to strike the right balance when configuring timeouts, as too short of a timeout could cause services to prematurely fail, while too long of a timeout could result in significant delays across the system.

Circuit breakers are another essential tool for building resilient microservices. A circuit breaker prevents a service from repeatedly trying to communicate with a service that is known to be failing, which could potentially exacerbate the problem. When a service repeatedly fails to respond, the circuit breaker trips and temporarily halts further communication with that service. This gives the failing service time to recover and reduces the load on the system. After a predetermined period, the circuit breaker allows attempts to access the service again, checking whether the issue has been resolved. By providing this mechanism, circuit breakers prevent cascading failures, where one service failure triggers a series of failures throughout the system.

In addition to retries, timeouts, and circuit breakers, microservices should also incorporate fallback mechanisms. A fallback is a predefined response or behavior that a service can take when it fails to communicate with another service. For example, if a service that processes payment transactions is unavailable, a fallback mechanism could return a cached response or provide a default response, ensuring that the user experience is not disrupted. This approach is particularly useful in situations where absolute real-time accuracy is not critical, and the system can still function with approximate or default data until the failing service becomes available again. Fallbacks help maintain the overall stability of the system by ensuring that certain operations can continue even when not all services are functioning as expected.

Another key aspect of fault tolerance is managing data consistency across services. In a microservices architecture, each service often has its own database, and data is typically replicated or shared between services to support business processes. Ensuring data consistency in such a distributed environment is a challenge, particularly when dealing with eventual consistency. Eventual consistency means that, over time, all services will converge on the same data state, but there may be periods where services have slightly different data. This inconsistency is usually acceptable as long as it does not lead to critical issues in the system. Techniques such as event sourcing, where changes to data are logged as events that can be replayed, and the Saga pattern, which breaks down long-running transactions into smaller, more manageable steps, can help manage this complexity and ensure that data consistency is eventually achieved.

In addition to handling failures within the system, microservices must be resilient to external failures, such as network failures or issues with third-party services. In such cases, external dependencies should be treated as potential points of failure. One way to build resilience in the face of external failures is by using timeouts and retries when interacting with external APIs or services. However, it is also essential to have contingency plans in place for when external services are unavailable for extended periods. For example, if an external payment service is down, the system might queue requests for processing later or temporarily provide alternative payment options. By building such contingencies into the architecture, the system can continue to function even in the face of external disruptions.

Monitoring and observability are critical for ensuring fault tolerance and resilience. In a distributed microservices system, it can be difficult to track the flow of requests and understand where failures are occurring. Distributed tracing allows developers to track a request as it travels through various services, providing visibility into how services interact and where bottlenecks or failures may occur. Tools like Jaeger, Zipkin, and OpenTelemetry provide distributed tracing capabilities, which can help teams identify issues and resolve them quickly. Additionally, centralized logging solutions such as the ELK stack (Elasticsearch, Logstash, Kibana) can aggregate logs from various services and provide a single point of reference for understanding system behavior. Metrics collection tools like Prometheus and Grafana help track performance metrics across services, enabling teams to monitor system health and identify any anomalies that may indicate impending failures.

Another important strategy for building resilience is to use redundancy and failover mechanisms. By deploying multiple instances of each microservice, the system can ensure high availability. If one instance of a service becomes unavailable, the load balancer can route traffic to another healthy instance. Similarly, when deploying microservices in a cloud environment or across multiple data centers, it is important to set up failover mechanisms that automatically redirect traffic to a backup instance in case of a failure. These redundancy and failover strategies ensure that the system remains operational even when individual components fail.

Ensuring fault tolerance and resilience in microservices requires careful planning and the implementation of several key strategies, including retries, timeouts, circuit breakers, fallbacks, and data consistency techniques. By employing these strategies and continuously monitoring system health, organizations can build microservices systems that are robust, reliable, and able to withstand failures without significant disruptions. Building resilience into the system not only helps maintain business continuity but also provides the flexibility and agility needed to respond to changes in traffic, demand, and failure conditions.

Caching Strategies in Microservices Systems

In a microservices architecture, where multiple independent services communicate with one another over a network, performance and efficiency can often be a concern. Each microservice typically has its own responsibilities and databases, and frequently interacting with these services can introduce significant latency. This can be especially problematic when services need to make repetitive or resource-intensive requests to fetch data. Caching is an essential strategy used in microservices systems to reduce latency, decrease load on databases, and enhance overall system performance. By storing frequently accessed data temporarily in a fast-access storage layer, caching minimizes the need to repeatedly fetch the same data from slower, more resource-intensive systems.

In a microservices environment, caching is typically implemented at multiple levels, depending on the specific needs and use cases of each service. One of the most common types of caching is data caching, which involves storing responses from a service in a cache to serve future requests more efficiently. When a client or service requests data, the system first checks whether the data is available in the cache. If it is, the data is served directly from the cache, significantly reducing response times. If the data is not in the cache, the request is forwarded to the underlying service or database, and the response is stored in the cache for subsequent use.

Caching can be implemented both on the client side and the server side, depending on the specific architecture of the microservices system. Client-side caching occurs when the client, such as a web browser or a mobile application, stores data locally. This approach is particularly useful for reducing the number of requests made to the server, particularly for static or rarely changing data. Server-side caching, on the other hand, involves storing data closer to the backend services, typically in a dedicated caching layer or database. This type of caching is useful for scenarios where many services require access to the same data or where data needs to be shared across multiple microservices.

Distributed caching is often used in microservices architectures where data needs to be shared between services. Since microservices are deployed independently, each service may run on different instances or even across multiple geographical regions. In such cases, it is important to have a shared cache that can be accessed by all services. Distributed caching systems like Redis, Memcached, or Hazelcast are commonly used for this purpose. These systems store cached data in memory, making it readily available to all services in the architecture. Distributed caches can be scaled horizontally to accommodate growing data and traffic demands, ensuring high availability and low-latency access to cached data. By providing a centralized cache accessible by multiple services, distributed caches eliminate the need for each service to maintain its own local cache, reducing redundancy and simplifying cache management.

Cache eviction is another important consideration when implementing caching strategies in microservices systems. Caches cannot hold an unlimited amount of data, so it is essential to define cache expiration policies to ensure that data remains relevant and does not consume unnecessary storage. Common eviction strategies include time-based expiration, where data is automatically removed from the cache after a certain period, and size-based eviction, where the cache is cleared once it reaches a predefined size. Another strategy is least-recently-used (LRU) eviction, which removes the least accessed items from the cache to make room for new data. The choice of eviction strategy depends on the specific use case and the nature of the data being cached. For example, if the cached data is highly dynamic and changes frequently, time-based expiration may be the most appropriate approach, while for static or long-lived data, size-based or LRU eviction may be more effective.

While caching can dramatically improve performance, it also introduces the challenge of ensuring data consistency. In a microservices architecture, different services may cache the same data, leading to situations where a cached value becomes outdated or inconsistent with the underlying data source. This can occur when data is updated in one service but the corresponding cache in another service is not updated. To handle this, cache invalidation mechanisms are employed to ensure that cached data remains consistent with the source of truth. Cache invalidation refers to the process of removing or updating cached data when the underlying data changes. One approach is to use write-through caching, where updates to the underlying database are immediately written to the cache. Another approach is write-behind caching, where updates to the cache are delayed until after the data has been written to the database. The choice between these strategies depends on the requirements of the application and the consistency guarantees needed.

Another important consideration is the trade-off between consistency and performance. In a distributed microservices system, it is often acceptable to allow some degree of inconsistency for the sake of performance. Eventual consistency is a concept that is often applied in caching strategies, where it is understood that cached data may be temporarily out of sync with the underlying data but will eventually be updated. Eventual consistency works well for scenarios where slight delays in data updates do not critically impact the system's functionality. For example, caching a product catalog for an e-commerce application can improve performance, and if the catalog is temporarily out of sync due to delayed cache updates, it will likely not have a significant impact on user experience.

Another caching strategy in microservices systems is the use of API caching. When a service relies on external APIs or third-party services, caching can be used to store the responses from these external calls. This helps reduce the dependency on external systems, which might be slower or subject to rate limits. API caching can be especially useful for services that rely on third-party APIs that provide data that doesn't change frequently. By caching the responses from these APIs at the microservice level, subsequent requests can be served from the cache rather than making additional API calls, thereby reducing latency and improving system efficiency.

Cache consistency also requires the use of synchronization mechanisms to ensure that updates are propagated correctly across different instances of the cache. In a distributed cache, different nodes may hold different versions of cached data, and updates to the data on one node need to be synchronized with all other nodes. This can be accomplished through techniques such as cache replication or distributed cache invalidation, where changes made to one node are propagated to others to maintain consistency across the system.

Security is another important consideration when implementing caching strategies in microservices. Caches may store sensitive data, and it is crucial to protect this data from unauthorized access. Caching systems should be configured to ensure that data is encrypted both at rest and in transit. Access to cached data should also be tightly controlled, with authentication and authorization mechanisms in place to prevent unauthorized access to cached resources.

Ultimately, the success of a caching strategy in microservices systems hinges on careful design and balancing performance, consistency, and complexity. By implementing appropriate caching mechanisms at various levels of the system—whether in the service layer, database layer, or API layer—organizations can improve the speed, responsiveness, and scalability of their microservices architectures. While caching introduces challenges such as cache invalidation, consistency, and security, these can be mitigated through well-designed caching strategies and robust infrastructure. When implemented effectively, caching enables microservices systems to deliver fast, reliable, and scalable services to end-users, contributing to a seamless and efficient user experience.

Logging and Monitoring in Microservices

In a microservices architecture, where services are distributed across multiple instances and communicate over a network, managing the health and performance of the system becomes a significant challenge. Traditional monolithic applications typically involve a single codebase and a centralized environment, which makes it easier to track logs, monitor performance, and diagnose issues. In contrast, microservices introduce complexity by breaking the application into independent services that operate in parallel, often across multiple servers or cloud environments. As the number of services increases, so does the complexity of tracking events, monitoring performance, and diagnosing failures. To address these challenges, logging and monitoring are essential components of any microservices architecture. These practices allow organizations to gain visibility into the behavior of services, ensure the reliability of the system, and quickly resolve issues when they arise.

Effective logging in a microservices architecture requires a comprehensive and consistent approach to capturing and managing logs across all services. Since each microservice is an independent unit of functionality, it often generates its own logs, which are specific to the operations and transactions handled by that service. Without proper coordination, these logs can quickly become fragmented, making it difficult to trace the flow of requests through the system and identify the source of issues. One of the most important strategies for managing logs in microservices is to use a centralized logging system. Centralized logging collects logs from all services in a single location, allowing developers and operations teams to access and analyze logs from multiple services in real time. Tools like the ELK stack (Elasticsearch, Logstash, and Kibana), Fluentd, and Graylog are commonly used for centralized logging in microservices environments. These tools aggregate logs from different services, parse them for meaningful data, and provide a unified interface for searching and analyzing logs.

In addition to centralizing logs, it is essential to ensure that logs are structured and standardized. Unstructured or inconsistent logs can make it difficult to gain useful insights into the behavior of the system. By using a structured logging format such as JSON, logs can be easily parsed and queried by automated tools. Structured logs typically include key pieces of information such as timestamps, service names, request identifiers, error codes, and context about the operation being performed. This structure enables teams to correlate logs from different services, track the flow of a request across multiple services, and identify the root cause of failures or performance issues. Logging frameworks like Logback, SLF4J, or Log4j allow for consistent logging across services, ensuring that all logs follow a predefined format and structure.

One of the most critical aspects of logging in microservices is the ability to trace a request as it moves through various services. Distributed tracing is a technique that allows for the tracking of a request across multiple microservices. Each service involved in processing the request adds its own trace information to the log, which can then be used to build a complete picture of the request's journey through the system. Distributed tracing systems, such as Jaeger, Zipkin, and OpenTelemetry, generate trace IDs that are passed along with each request. These trace IDs help link together logs from different services, allowing teams to trace the flow of a single request across service boundaries and identify performance bottlenecks or errors. Distributed tracing provides valuable insights into the performance of individual services and helps pinpoint where delays or failures are occurring.

In addition to logging, monitoring is a key component of maintaining the health and performance of a microservices system. Monitoring involves continuously tracking the performance metrics of each service, such as response times, error rates, and resource usage. This provides a real-time view of the system's health and helps identify potential issues before they impact users. In a microservices architecture, monitoring must be comprehensive and include both infrastructure-level monitoring (e.g., CPU usage, memory consumption) and application-level monitoring (e.g., request counts, latency). Tools like Prometheus, Grafana, and Datadog are widely used to collect and visualize metrics from microservices systems. Prometheus, for example, scrapes metrics from services that expose them through HTTP endpoints, while Grafana provides powerful visualization capabilities, allowing teams to create dashboards that display key performance indicators (KPIs) in real time.

One important aspect of monitoring is setting up alerting mechanisms that notify teams when certain thresholds are exceeded. For example, if the error rate for a service exceeds a predefined threshold, or if the response time becomes too slow, an alert can be triggered to notify the relevant team. Alerts help ensure that issues are addressed proactively before they lead to more serious problems, such as downtime or customer impact. Alerting systems like PagerDuty, Opsgenie, or Slack integrations can notify on-call engineers, ensuring that they respond to issues promptly. The key to effective alerting is ensuring that alerts are meaningful and actionable. Too many alerts or poorly configured alerts can lead to alert fatigue, where important issues are overlooked due to the volume of notifications.

An essential consideration when monitoring microservices is the handling of high cardinality metrics. Microservices systems often generate a large number of unique metrics, such as request identifiers, user IDs, or transaction IDs, which can result in a massive volume of data. Monitoring tools must be capable of managing high cardinality metrics efficiently to avoid performance degradation. One approach to handling high cardinality metrics is to aggregate or sample the data, collecting only the most important or representative information. For example, rather than tracking every individual user's request, a system might track metrics for request counts across different regions or services. This reduces the amount of data that needs to be processed and stored while still providing valuable insights into system performance.

Log management and monitoring tools are not only important for identifying issues but also for gaining insights into system behavior and performance trends over time. By analyzing historical data, teams can detect patterns, anticipate future needs, and make informed decisions about scaling, infrastructure changes, or code optimizations. For example, monitoring tools can help identify which services experience the highest load, enabling teams to prioritize scaling efforts or optimize those services for better performance. Similarly, by analyzing logs and metrics together, teams can gain a deeper understanding of how different services interact and identify areas for optimization.

In addition to traditional monitoring and logging practices, microservices systems can benefit from implementing advanced observability techniques. Observability refers to the ability to measure and understand the internal state of a system based on the data it generates. This includes not only logs and metrics but also other forms of telemetry, such as traces and events. By integrating observability practices, teams can gain a holistic view of system behavior and performance. For example, combining metrics with traces allows teams to pinpoint exactly where bottlenecks occur in the flow of requests and determine which services are causing delays. This level of observability is critical in a microservices environment, where distributed systems can hide problems that are difficult to detect without comprehensive monitoring and logging.

Logging and monitoring are essential practices for maintaining the health, performance, and reliability of a microservices system. By implementing centralized logging, structured logs, and distributed tracing, organizations can gain deep visibility into their services and quickly identify and address issues. Effective monitoring, combined with alerting and high cardinality management, helps ensure that services perform optimally, even in the face of scaling challenges. With the right tools and strategies, logging and monitoring can help microservices systems remain resilient, responsive, and capable of handling the complexities of distributed architectures.

Distributed Tracing for Microservices

As organizations move toward microservices architectures, managing the complexity of distributed systems becomes an increasingly important challenge. Microservices, by nature, involve a large number of independently deployable services that communicate with one another over a network, which can lead to difficulties in understanding how data flows through the system and identifying performance bottlenecks or failures. Distributed tracing is a powerful technique used to address these challenges by providing detailed visibility into the flow of requests as they move through multiple services. Distributed tracing enables teams to track the lifecycle of a request across a system, offering valuable insights into performance, latency, and potential points of failure, which are critical for maintaining the health and efficiency of microservices architectures.

At its core, distributed tracing involves tracking a request as it travels through various microservices in a system. When a client makes a request, it is processed by one service, which may need to call additional services to complete the task. Each service involved in processing the request generates trace data that is collected and correlated to provide a comprehensive view of the request's journey across the system. Distributed tracing enables teams to understand how individual services interact, where delays occur, and which services are most affected by high traffic or resource constraints. This ability to track and analyze the flow of requests across different services is invaluable in diagnosing performance issues, understanding dependencies, and optimizing microservices architectures.

The fundamental unit of distributed tracing is a trace, which represents a single request that flows through the system. A trace is composed of multiple spans, each representing an individual service or operation within the system. For example, a trace might include a span for the initial request to the API gateway, followed by spans for each microservice that processes the request, such as authentication, payment processing, or data retrieval. Each span includes information such as the start and end times, the service name, and any metadata associated with the request. The span also includes a trace ID, which allows the spans to be correlated across services to form a complete view of the request's journey.

Distributed tracing systems use these trace IDs to link spans together, even if they are generated by different services running on different machines. This allows teams to see how a single request flows through the entire system, from the frontend to the backend, across multiple microservices. By visualizing these traces, developers and operations teams can pinpoint which services are taking the longest to respond, where errors are occurring, and where bottlenecks are introduced. For example, if a trace reveals that a request is delayed significantly due to a slow database query in one service, teams can focus their efforts on optimizing that particular service or database operation, improving overall performance.

One of the main benefits of distributed tracing is its ability to provide end-to-end visibility into a system that spans multiple services and components. In traditional monolithic systems, performance monitoring is often simpler because all components reside in the same codebase and interact directly with one another. In contrast, microservices systems can be much more complex, with services running on different machines, containers, or cloud environments. Distributed tracing makes it possible to trace the path of requests through these distributed environments, helping to break down the silos between services and providing a unified view of system performance.

A key aspect of distributed tracing is the ability to monitor the latency between different services. When a request passes through multiple microservices, it is common for each service to introduce some level of latency, whether due to network communication, processing time, or resource contention. By tracking the time spent in each service, distributed tracing allows teams to identify which services are contributing the most to overall latency. This is especially useful for optimizing performance in high-traffic systems, where even small delays in one service can lead to significant slowdowns across the entire system. By pinpointing these latency hotspots, teams can prioritize optimizations that have the greatest impact on system performance.

In addition to latency monitoring, distributed tracing also helps to identify errors and failures that occur in the system. In a distributed microservices architecture, a failure in one service can cascade and affect other services that depend on it. Without distributed tracing, it can be difficult to identify the root cause of such failures, as the failure may be masked by the chain of service interactions. With tracing, however, teams can see exactly where the failure occurred and which services were involved. For example, if a request to the payment service fails due to an internal error, distributed tracing allows teams to trace the failure back to the service that caused it, providing clear context for debugging and resolution.

Another important benefit of distributed tracing is its ability to assist in understanding dependencies between services. In a microservices architecture, services often depend on one another to complete business transactions. For instance, an order service may depend on inventory, payment, and shipping services to process an order. By visualizing the dependencies between services, distributed tracing allows teams to identify potential risks or weak points in the system. For example, if the inventory service is frequently slow or unreliable, it could affect the performance of all services that rely on it. Distributed tracing helps highlight these dependencies, allowing teams to optimize or even decouple services to reduce the impact of failure in critical components.

Distributed tracing systems often integrate with other observability tools, such as logging and metrics systems, to provide a more comprehensive picture of system health. Logs capture detailed information about specific events or errors, while metrics track high-level performance indicators such as request counts, response times, and resource utilization. By correlating trace data with logs and metrics, teams can gain deeper insights into system performance and identify the root causes of issues more effectively. For example, if a trace shows a performance bottleneck, developers can check the logs for any errors or anomalies that might be contributing to the delay, and they can monitor the related metrics to see if the issue is tied to resource utilization, such as high CPU or memory usage.

There are several tools available for implementing distributed tracing in microservices systems. OpenTelemetry is an open-source framework that provides libraries and APIs for instrumenting code and collecting trace data. It can be integrated with various backend systems, such as Jaeger, Zipkin, or Prometheus, which store, visualize, and analyze trace data. These tools offer powerful features for tracing and visualizing the flow of requests, identifying performance bottlenecks, and diagnosing errors. While distributed tracing can introduce some overhead, especially in high-volume systems, modern tracing systems are designed to be lightweight and efficient, ensuring that the benefits of tracing far outweigh the performance cost.

As microservices systems grow in size and complexity, the ability to monitor and optimize them becomes more critical. Distributed tracing provides a powerful mechanism for gaining deep visibility into a system, helping teams identify performance bottlenecks, track the flow of requests, and troubleshoot issues. By visualizing the journey of requests across multiple services, distributed tracing enables teams to understand how individual services interact and how failures propagate through the system. This level of visibility is crucial for maintaining the health and performance of microservices architectures, ensuring that systems are both efficient and resilient in the face of increasing complexity.

Testing Microservices: Approaches and Tools

Testing in a microservices architecture presents unique challenges and requires a strategic approach to ensure the system works as intended. Unlike monolithic applications, where testing can be more straightforward due to the system's single codebase, microservices consist of independent, loosely coupled services that interact through APIs or messaging queues. These services are deployed independently, often across multiple environments, and may even be written in different programming languages. As a result, traditional testing methods are not sufficient for verifying that the system functions correctly as a whole. Instead, testing in microservices must be comprehensive, covering various levels of the system, including individual services, their interactions, and the system as a whole. A combination of different testing approaches and specialized tools is required to effectively validate the behavior, performance, and resilience of microservices architectures.

The first and most fundamental level of testing in microservices is unit testing. Unit tests are designed to validate the functionality of individual components within a microservice. These tests are typically isolated from the rest of the system and focus on testing the logic of specific functions or methods. Unit testing is crucial because it ensures that the individual building blocks of a microservice are working as expected before they are integrated into the broader system. Frameworks like JUnit for Java, Mocha for Node.js, or pytest for Python are commonly used for unit testing, allowing developers to write automated tests that can be run frequently during development. By catching issues at the unit level, developers can prevent bugs from propagating to other parts of the system, ensuring that each microservice remains robust and reliable.

Once individual services have been unit-tested, the next step is to conduct integration testing. Integration tests verify that the different components within a microservice, such as the database, external APIs, and internal services, interact correctly. Since microservices often rely on other services for functionality, integration testing is crucial for ensuring that these dependencies work as expected when the services are combined. These tests focus on checking the behavior of the microservice when it interacts with real-world components like databases, message queues, or other microservices. Integration testing can also help verify that the service's API endpoints are functioning correctly and returning the expected responses. Tools like Postman, RestAssured, or Supertest can be used to automate API testing during integration testing, ensuring that services are properly integrated and that their communication flows smoothly.

One of the challenges in microservices testing is the need to test how services interact with each other. Since microservices are distributed across different nodes or containers, it is not always feasible to run all services in a test environment during integration testing. This is where contract testing comes into play. Contract testing ensures that the communication between services remains consistent and reliable. In a contract test, a service is tested against the contract or specification that defines how it should interact with other services. This type of testing verifies that services can communicate with each other without breaking the contract, even if one of the services is modified. Tools like Pact and Spring Cloud Contract provide frameworks for implementing contract testing, ensuring that microservices adhere to the expected interfaces and behave as intended during interactions.

End-to-end testing is another critical approach in microservices testing. End-to-end tests verify that the entire system, including all of its services and their interactions, functions as expected. These tests simulate real user behavior and validate that the microservices ecosystem works as a cohesive whole. End-to-end testing is particularly important in microservices because it tests the integration of services and ensures that they are not only working individually but also collaborating effectively. Since microservices systems often involve complex workflows with multiple services interacting with one another, end-to-end tests help ensure that data flows correctly across services and that the business logic is correctly implemented. However, due to the complexity of testing across multiple services, end-to-end tests can be time-consuming and resource-intensive. To mitigate this, many organizations use service virtualization techniques, where mock versions of external services are used to simulate interactions with the rest of the system during testing.

One of the more advanced testing strategies in microservices is chaos testing. Chaos testing focuses on testing the resilience of the system by intentionally introducing failures into the environment. This type of testing helps to verify that the system can handle unexpected disruptions and that services can recover gracefully from failures. By simulating scenarios like service crashes, network latency, or hardware failures, chaos testing ensures that microservices remain resilient and that the system as a whole continues to operate despite individual failures. Tools like Gremlin or Chaos Monkey (from Netflix) are commonly used to implement chaos testing, allowing teams to inject faults and simulate failure scenarios in a controlled manner. This approach is particularly valuable in highly distributed environments, where the likelihood of failure is inherent, and resilience is critical to maintaining system stability and reliability.

In addition to testing the functionality and resilience of microservices, performance testing is also a crucial part of the testing process. Performance tests ensure that the system can handle the expected load and that it meets performance requirements such as response times, throughput, and resource utilization. In a microservices architecture, performance testing must consider the interactions between services, as bottlenecks can occur when multiple services are involved in processing a single request. Load testing, stress testing, and scalability testing are essential techniques for validating the performance of microservices. Tools like Apache JMeter, Gatling, and Artillery are commonly used to simulate high levels of traffic and measure how the system performs under load. Performance testing helps identify potential bottlenecks, scalability issues, or resource constraints before they impact the system in production.

In modern microservices environments, automated testing is a key component of the development lifecycle. Continuous integration and continuous delivery (CI/CD) pipelines are often used to automate testing, ensuring that each microservice is thoroughly tested before being deployed to production. Automated testing reduces the manual effort required to run tests and enables teams to catch issues earlier in the development process. By integrating testing into the CI/CD pipeline, microservices teams can continuously validate the integrity of the system, ensuring that new features or changes do not introduce bugs or regressions. Tools like Jenkins, GitLab CI, and CircleCI are commonly used to automate the testing and deployment process, enabling rapid feedback and faster development cycles.

To complement automated testing, monitoring tools play a crucial role in ensuring that microservices are functioning as expected in production. Monitoring provides real-time insights into the health and performance of the system, allowing teams to detect issues and respond quickly. Metrics such as request rates, error rates, and latency are monitored to ensure that the system is performing optimally. Tools like Prometheus, Grafana, and Datadog help teams track these metrics and alert them to any anomalies. Monitoring also helps to continuously validate the performance and stability of microservices after they have been deployed, ensuring that the system continues to meet business requirements.

Testing microservices requires a comprehensive strategy that covers different levels, from unit testing individual services to end-to-end testing the entire system. By using a combination of testing approaches, such as contract testing, chaos testing, performance testing, and automated testing, teams can ensure that microservices work reliably and efficiently both individually and as part of the overall system. The use of specialized tools like Postman, Pact, Jenkins, and Prometheus, along with a well-structured testing pipeline, enables teams to manage the complexities of microservices testing and maintain the stability and reliability of the system. As microservices continue to grow in popularity, effective testing will remain an essential component of ensuring that these systems deliver high-quality, scalable, and resilient applications.

CI/CD Pipelines for Microservices

In a microservices architecture, the process of software delivery and deployment can become more complex compared to traditional monolithic applications. Microservices are independent, modular units of functionality that interact with one another via APIs or messaging systems. This distributed nature, while providing flexibility, scalability, and agility, also requires efficient processes for continuous integration (CI) and continuous delivery (CD). CI/CD pipelines are crucial for managing the development, testing, and deployment of microservices, ensuring that changes are delivered quickly, reliably, and with minimal risk. By automating the stages of the software lifecycle, CI/CD pipelines help teams maintain a high level of efficiency while minimizing manual errors and downtime.

Continuous integration (CI) is the practice of frequently integrating code changes into a shared repository. In a microservices environment, this means that developers from different teams can submit changes to their respective services. Each time a change is made to a service, it is automatically built and tested. This practice allows teams to detect issues early in the development cycle, reducing the chances of integration problems and making it easier to identify bugs and vulnerabilities before they escalate. Automated tests, such as unit tests and integration tests, are an integral part of the CI process, ensuring that each microservice behaves as expected after changes are introduced. CI helps maintain the stability of the system by continuously verifying the correctness of individual services, ensuring that they can interact with other services smoothly.

For microservices, continuous delivery (CD) extends CI by automating the deployment process. Once code has been integrated and passed through automated tests, it is automatically deployed to various environments, such as staging and production. The key benefit of CD is that it enables rapid, consistent, and reliable deployments, with minimal downtime and disruption to end-users. In a microservices-based system, services are often deployed independently, which allows for faster and more flexible deployments compared to traditional monolithic applications. This independence is one of the core advantages of microservices, and CD pipelines are designed to support this by automating the deployment of individual services or groups of services without requiring the entire system to be redeployed.

A CI/CD pipeline for microservices typically involves several stages that automate tasks such as code compilation, testing, artifact creation, and deployment. Each stage ensures that the service is thoroughly validated before it is released to the next stage. For instance, the first stage might involve compiling the source code and building a container image, which is then pushed to a container registry. Following that, the pipeline might run a series of automated tests, including unit tests, integration tests, and static code analysis, to ensure that the service meets the required standards for functionality and security. If the service passes all tests, it is then deployed to a staging environment, where further automated tests can be run in an environment that closely mirrors production.

One of the challenges of CI/CD in microservices is handling the complexities of managing multiple independent services. Unlike monolithic applications, where a single codebase is compiled and deployed, microservices often involve numerous services, each with its own codebase, database, and set of dependencies. Coordinating the deployment of these services can be complicated, especially when services have dependencies on each other. For instance, a change in one service might require changes to several other services, and testing and deploying those services in isolation might not be sufficient. In such cases, CI/CD pipelines must be able to manage these dependencies and ensure that changes are deployed in the correct order, while maintaining the autonomy of each service.

To manage dependencies effectively, a microservices CI/CD pipeline often incorporates service discovery and container orchestration tools like Kubernetes. These tools help automate the scaling, management, and deployment of services in production environments. Kubernetes, for example, allows services to be deployed as containers in pods, which can be easily scaled and managed based on traffic demands. It also supports rolling updates, which allow services to be updated without downtime. With Kubernetes, each microservice can be deployed independently, but the system as a whole can remain highly available, even during deployments or failures. Additionally, Kubernetes can manage service-to-service communication, ensuring that services can locate and interact with each other even as they scale and change.

Another important consideration when implementing CI/CD pipelines for microservices is the need for version control and backward compatibility. Since microservices evolve over time, it is crucial that new versions of services can coexist with older versions. One of the challenges in microservices systems is maintaining compatibility between different versions of services. For example, if one service relies on data from another service, a change to the API of the second service could break functionality in the first. To address this, teams typically implement versioning strategies for APIs and maintain backward compatibility between services. In a CI/CD pipeline, this means that versioning must be carefully managed during deployment, ensuring that older versions of services are supported until the new versions are fully tested and deployed.

Testing is a fundamental component of CI/CD pipelines in microservices, especially considering the high degree of inter-service communication. Automated tests ensure that services remain functional after every change, but testing can be more complex in distributed systems. For example, unit tests validate individual services, while integration tests ensure that multiple services can work together. However, because services are deployed independently, there is always the possibility that changes to one service could affect the functionality of others. To address this, CI/CD pipelines for microservices should include end-to-end testing that simulates real-world use cases, testing the interactions between services in a production-like environment. This is particularly important for microservices systems, where the failure of one service can have a cascading effect on the entire system.

Incorporating automated monitoring and rollback capabilities into CI/CD pipelines is another key consideration for microservices systems. Since microservices are often deployed in dynamic environments, it is essential to ensure that any issues that arise during deployment are quickly identified and addressed. Automated monitoring tools, such as Prometheus or Datadog, can track key performance indicators (KPIs) during deployment, helping to detect issues such as increased latency, errors, or system outages. Additionally, CI/CD pipelines should include automated rollback mechanisms that can revert a service to its previous version if a deployment causes problems. This minimizes the impact of failures and helps maintain the stability of the system.

One of the advantages of using CI/CD pipelines in microservices is the ability to implement continuous testing and delivery without compromising the agility and autonomy of individual services. Since microservices are independent, each service can have its own CI/CD pipeline, tailored to its specific needs. This autonomy allows teams to deploy and release changes independently, reducing the time it takes to bring new features to market and making it easier to maintain the overall system. At the same time, by automating the testing and deployment process, CI/CD pipelines ensure that services are consistently delivered with a high level of quality and reliability.

CI/CD pipelines are an essential part of managing and deploying microservices architectures. By automating the testing, building, and deployment of services, CI/CD pipelines enable teams to deliver high-quality services quickly and reliably. While microservices introduce complexity due to their distributed nature, CI/CD tools like Kubernetes, Jenkins, and GitLab CI help manage these complexities by providing automated workflows that streamline development and deployment processes. By implementing these pipelines, organizations can ensure that their microservices systems remain agile, scalable, and resilient, capable of handling rapid change while maintaining high levels of performance and reliability.

Managing and Automating Microservices Deployments

Managing and automating microservices deployments is a crucial aspect of ensuring the efficiency, scalability, and reliability of microservices architectures. Microservices are designed to be independently deployable, meaning that each service operates in its own environment, often with its own codebase, database, and deployment pipeline. This autonomy is one of the defining characteristics of microservices, allowing teams to develop, test, and deploy services independently. However, this independence also introduces challenges in managing deployments at scale. The complexity of coordinating the deployment of multiple services, handling dependencies, ensuring continuous availability, and maintaining a smooth user experience requires robust management and automation strategies.

The first step in managing microservices deployments effectively is to establish clear, automated processes for building, testing, and deploying each service. Microservices are often built in containers, which provide a consistent and portable runtime environment. By containerizing services, teams can ensure that each service runs reliably across different environments, from development to production. Containerization also enables rapid and consistent deployments, as services can be packaged with all of their dependencies into a single unit. Tools like Docker are commonly used for containerizing microservices, while container orchestration platforms like Kubernetes help manage the deployment, scaling, and operation of containers in production environments.

Kubernetes plays a central role in automating microservices deployments, providing a platform for automating container management. It abstracts away much of the complexity of deploying and managing containers, allowing teams to focus on building and scaling services rather than worrying about low-level infrastructure management. Kubernetes enables declarative configurations, where the desired state of the system is defined in configuration files, and it automatically adjusts the system to match that state. For instance, teams can define how many instances of a service should be running, and Kubernetes will ensure that the specified number of instances is maintained, automatically scaling the service up or down as needed. This level of automation is particularly beneficial in dynamic, cloud-native environments where services must scale based on varying levels of demand.

In addition to container orchestration, microservices deployments require continuous integration and continuous delivery (CI/CD) pipelines to automate the entire process from code commit to deployment. CI/CD pipelines are essential for managing microservices deployments at scale, as they enable teams to automate the build, test, and deployment stages of development. When a developer commits changes to a microservice, the CI/CD pipeline automatically builds the service, runs unit and integration tests, and deploys it to a staging environment for further testing. If the service passes all tests, the pipeline automatically deploys the service to production, ensuring that updates are delivered consistently and reliably. Tools like Jenkins, GitLab CI, and CircleCI are commonly used to automate these workflows, providing a seamless process for developers to deliver new features and bug fixes.

Managing microservices deployments also involves handling service dependencies, which can be particularly complex in a distributed system. Unlike monolithic applications, where components share the same environment and database, microservices interact through APIs or messaging systems, with each service potentially depending on others. This introduces the challenge of managing dependencies between services during deployments. To handle this complexity, teams often use service discovery mechanisms and API gateways to ensure that services can locate and communicate with each other as needed. Service discovery tools, such as Consul or Eureka, allow services to register themselves and automatically find other services in the system, enabling dynamic communication even as services are scaled up or down. API gateways, such as Kong or Nginx, provide a centralized entry point for external requests, routing them to the appropriate services and managing cross-cutting concerns like authentication, rate limiting, and logging.

To minimize downtime during deployments, teams often adopt rolling updates and blue-green deployment strategies. Rolling updates involve gradually updating instances of a service while ensuring that the rest of the system remains available. In this approach, a new version of a service is deployed alongside the old version, and traffic is progressively shifted to the new version as it becomes available. This allows teams to update services without taking the entire system offline and provides an opportunity to roll back the update if issues arise. Blue-green deployments, on the other hand, involve deploying the new version of a service in parallel with the old version in a separate environment (the "blue" and "green" environments). Once the new version is fully tested and ready, traffic is switched over from the old version to the new version, minimizing downtime and ensuring that the system remains available throughout the process.

Another challenge in managing microservices deployments is ensuring that the system remains resilient in the face of failures. Given that microservices are distributed across multiple nodes, there is always the potential for failures in individual services, containers, or infrastructure components. To address this, teams must implement fault tolerance and recovery mechanisms that allow the system to remain operational even when components fail. One common approach is to use circuit breakers, which prevent a failing service from causing cascading failures throughout the system. A circuit breaker monitors the health of a service and, if it detects repeated failures, temporarily halts communication with the service, allowing it time to recover. Once the service is healthy again, the circuit breaker is closed, and communication resumes. Tools like Hystrix or Resilience4j provide libraries for implementing circuit breakers in microservices systems.

Monitoring and observability are also essential aspects of managing and automating microservices deployments. As the number of services grows, it becomes increasingly difficult to track the health and performance of the system without proper monitoring. Tools like Prometheus, Grafana, and Datadog can be used to collect and visualize metrics such as response times, error rates, and resource utilization across microservices. These metrics help teams monitor the performance of individual services and the overall system, providing insights into potential issues before they impact users. Distributed tracing tools like Jaeger or Zipkin allow teams to trace requests as they flow through different services, helping to identify performance bottlenecks or failures in the system. By collecting logs, metrics, and traces in a centralized location, teams can gain visibility into the behavior of the entire system and respond quickly to any issues that arise.

Automating microservices deployments also requires robust security measures to ensure that services are deployed safely and that sensitive data is protected. Security best practices, such as using secure communication protocols (e.g., HTTPS, TLS), implementing authentication and authorization mechanisms (e.g., OAuth 2.0, JWT), and regularly scanning containers for vulnerabilities, should be integrated into the CI/CD pipeline. Tools like Docker Content Trust and Clair can be used to scan container images for known vulnerabilities, while security policies can be enforced through tools like Kubernetes Network Policies or Istio. By automating security checks as part of the deployment process, teams can reduce the risk of deploying vulnerable or insecure services into production.

Managing and automating microservices deployments involves orchestrating services, automating build and deployment processes, handling service dependencies, ensuring resilience, and maintaining observability. With the help of container orchestration tools like Kubernetes, CI/CD pipelines, service discovery mechanisms, and fault tolerance techniques, teams can deploy microservices quickly, efficiently, and with minimal risk. Automating deployments also enables teams to continuously deliver new features, improvements, and bug fixes while maintaining high levels of availability and performance. By integrating security and monitoring practices into the deployment process, organizations can ensure that their microservices systems are both resilient and secure, capable of supporting dynamic, large-scale applications.

Containerization of Microservices with Docker

Containerization has become one of the cornerstones of modern software development, particularly in microservices architectures. Microservices, which decompose applications into smaller, independent services, bring a significant degree of flexibility and scalability. However, managing and deploying these services, especially in production environments, can become complex due to the dependencies, configurations, and environments each service requires. This is where containerization, specifically using Docker, plays a vital role. Docker allows developers to package applications and their dependencies into a standardized unit known as a container. These containers are lightweight, portable, and can run consistently across different environments, making Docker an ideal solution for deploying microservices.

The fundamental concept behind Docker and containerization is the ability to isolate an application, along with all of its dependencies, into a single, self-contained unit. Unlike traditional virtual machines, which require a full operating system to run each application, containers share the host operating system's kernel but run in isolated environments. This makes containers much more efficient in terms of resource usage, as they are lightweight and start up quickly. For microservices, which often involve deploying multiple instances of different services, Docker provides an effective way to package and deploy these services while ensuring they run consistently across various environments, from development to testing and production.

With Docker, each microservice can be packaged into its own container, which includes not only the application code but also all the libraries, frameworks, and configurations that the service needs to run. This eliminates the "works on my machine" problem, where an application runs on one developer's local machine but fails to run on others due to differences in environments or dependencies. By using containers, developers can be confident that the application will behave the same way in all environments, ensuring greater consistency and reducing the chances of environment-related issues when deploying to production.

Docker also provides a simple way to define and manage containers using a configuration file known as a Dockerfile. This file describes the steps required to build a container, including which base image to use, which dependencies need to be installed, and how the application should be executed. A Dockerfile allows developers to define repeatable build processes for containers, ensuring that every instance of a service is built consistently and according to the same specifications. This level of automation simplifies the development and deployment pipeline, especially in a microservices environment, where multiple services need to be deployed independently and often need to scale in response to varying traffic demands.

One of the major benefits of containerization with Docker is portability. Containers can be deployed on any system that has Docker installed, whether it's a developer's laptop, a staging server, or a cloud-based infrastructure. This portability makes Docker particularly well-suited for microservices architectures, where services are often distributed across multiple environments. Whether running on a local machine, a virtual machine, or a cloud platform like AWS, Azure, or Google Cloud, containers ensure that each service is packaged in a way that it will run consistently, without requiring specific configuration adjustments for each environment. This greatly simplifies the deployment process and enhances the flexibility of the architecture.

In a microservices architecture, Docker is typically used in conjunction with container orchestration tools such as Kubernetes. Kubernetes provides automated deployment, scaling, and management of containerized applications, helping to manage the complexity of running large numbers of containers in production environments. When using Docker with Kubernetes, each microservice runs in its own container, and Kubernetes manages the scheduling, scaling, and health checks of these containers across clusters of machines. Kubernetes allows for dynamic scaling of microservices, meaning that as demand increases for a particular service, additional instances of the container can be spun up automatically, ensuring the system can handle traffic spikes without manual intervention.

Containerization with Docker also facilitates continuous integration and continuous delivery (CI/CD) practices in microservices architectures. In CI/CD pipelines, Docker containers can be used to automate the build, test, and deployment stages of the software development lifecycle. When a developer makes changes to a microservice, the CI pipeline automatically builds a new Docker image from the updated code, runs tests to verify functionality, and then pushes the updated image to a container registry. From there, the CD pipeline automatically deploys the new container to a staging or production environment. This process ensures that new features, bug fixes, or updates are delivered quickly and consistently, while also reducing the risk of human error during deployment.

Furthermore, Docker's ability to create isolated environments for each microservice helps improve security. Each container runs in its own isolated environment, ensuring that services cannot interfere with one another. In a microservices architecture, where services may be running on different machines or containers, this isolation adds an extra layer of security by preventing one service from accessing the resources of another. Docker also allows for setting resource limits for each container, such as CPU and memory usage, which can help prevent any single service from consuming too many resources and affecting the performance of others.

Despite its many advantages, Docker also requires careful management in large-scale microservices environments. As the number of services grows, so does the number of containers, and managing them manually can become difficult. This is where container orchestration tools like Kubernetes become essential. Kubernetes provides a centralized way to manage containerized microservices, ensuring that they are deployed, scaled, and monitored efficiently. With Kubernetes, developers can define the desired state of the system using configuration files, and Kubernetes automatically adjusts the system to match that state, handling tasks such as container scheduling, load balancing, and self-healing in the event of failures.

Logging and monitoring are also crucial when using Docker for microservices. Since each service runs in its own container, traditional methods of logging and monitoring may not be sufficient. Docker provides built-in logging drivers that allow logs to be captured and centralized for easy analysis. Tools like the ELK stack (Elasticsearch, Logstash, and Kibana) or Prometheus and Grafana can be integrated with Docker to aggregate logs and metrics from containers, giving developers visibility into the performance and behavior of each service. Monitoring tools can also track container resource usage, helping to identify performance bottlenecks or failures before they impact users.

Docker has become an integral part of managing and deploying microservices in modern software architectures. Its ability to package services and their dependencies into portable, isolated containers simplifies the process of deploying microservices across different environments. Docker, combined with container orchestration tools like Kubernetes, provides a scalable, flexible, and automated approach to managing microservices deployments, ensuring that services are deployed quickly, reliably, and securely. By leveraging containerization with Docker, teams can reduce the complexity of managing microservices and improve the efficiency and consistency of the development, testing, and deployment pipelines.

Orchestration with Kubernetes for Microservices

In a microservices architecture, each service is designed to be independently deployable, scalable, and capable of functioning autonomously. However, managing a large number of independent microservices can quickly become a complex task, especially when considering factors like service discovery, load balancing, scaling, networking, and fault tolerance. This complexity is where Kubernetes, a powerful container orchestration tool, comes into play. Kubernetes enables teams to automate the deployment, scaling, and management of containerized applications, providing the tools needed to handle the operational complexity inherent in microservices environments. Through Kubernetes, microservices can be deployed in a way that is highly available, resilient, and scalable, making it an essential tool for managing modern cloud-native applications.

Kubernetes was originally developed by Google to manage large-scale containerized applications, and it has since become the industry standard for orchestrating containers in production environments. The primary goal of Kubernetes is to abstract away the complexity of managing containers, allowing developers to focus on building applications while Kubernetes handles the underlying infrastructure. Kubernetes provides a set of robust features for automating the deployment, scaling, and management of microservices, making it a natural fit for microservices architectures.

One of the key features of Kubernetes is its ability to automate the deployment and management of containers. When a microservice is containerized using Docker, Kubernetes allows that container to be run on any infrastructure—whether on-premises or in the cloud—without modification. Kubernetes orchestrates the deployment of containers across a cluster of machines, ensuring that each container runs in the right place and that resources are allocated efficiently. This eliminates the need for developers to manually manage the distribution of containers across servers, and it provides greater flexibility by allowing microservices to be deployed on any type of environment that supports Kubernetes.

Kubernetes also excels in managing the scaling of microservices. In a microservices architecture, different services may have varying demands based on the workload, and some services may need to scale up or down independently of others. Kubernetes provides horizontal scaling, which allows services to scale by increasing or decreasing the number of container instances running at any given time. Kubernetes can automatically scale microservices in response to real-time traffic, adjusting the number of running containers based on predefined metrics, such as CPU usage or memory consumption. This dynamic scaling capability ensures that the system can handle spikes in traffic without manual intervention, and it helps optimize resource usage by scaling down services during periods of low demand.

In addition to scaling, Kubernetes facilitates high availability and fault tolerance. Microservices architectures are often deployed in distributed environments, which inherently increases the risk of service failures. Kubernetes mitigates this risk by providing features such as replication and self-healing. Each service in Kubernetes can be replicated across multiple instances (or pods) to ensure that there are always healthy instances of the service running. If one instance of a service fails, Kubernetes automatically redeploys it or switches traffic to healthy replicas, ensuring that the service remains available. This self-healing capability is crucial in microservices environments, where the failure of a single service should not lead to downtime for the entire system. By maintaining replicas and managing the availability of services, Kubernetes ensures that the microservices architecture remains resilient and fault-tolerant.

Service discovery is another challenge that Kubernetes addresses for microservices. In traditional monolithic applications, services can communicate directly through shared memory or local network connections. However, in a distributed microservices architecture, services are often deployed on different machines or containers, making it difficult to keep track of their locations. Kubernetes provides built-in service discovery, allowing services to automatically register themselves and find other services within the cluster. When a new instance of a service is deployed, Kubernetes updates the service registry, and other services can query this registry to find the location of the new instance. This automated service discovery simplifies communication between microservices and ensures that services can always find each other, even as they scale or fail over time.

Load balancing is a critical feature for any microservices system, as services must efficiently distribute incoming traffic across multiple instances to ensure that no single instance is overwhelmed. Kubernetes provides automatic load balancing for services through a feature known as the Service resource. When a service is exposed in Kubernetes, it is assigned a stable IP address and DNS name that can be used by other services to communicate with it. Kubernetes automatically distributes incoming requests to the different instances of the service, ensuring that traffic is balanced and that no instance is overloaded. This load balancing mechanism ensures that microservices can handle high volumes of traffic without performance degradation.

Another advantage of using Kubernetes for microservices orchestration is its robust networking capabilities. Kubernetes manages the communication between services using a flat network model, where every pod (container instance) can communicate with every other pod in the cluster, regardless of the underlying infrastructure. This simplifies the networking model for microservices, as developers do not need to manually configure network routes or firewalls for service communication. Kubernetes also provides the ability to set up network policies, enabling fine-grained control over the communication between services. For example, you can configure Kubernetes to allow only certain services to communicate with each other, enhancing security by isolating sensitive services from the rest of the system.

Kubernetes also plays a significant role in the management of configurations and secrets. In a microservices architecture, services often require configuration data, such as database connection strings, API keys, or other sensitive information. Kubernetes provides resources such as ConfigMaps and Secrets to manage this configuration data in a secure and organized manner. ConfigMaps allow you to store non-sensitive configuration data that can be injected into containers at runtime, while Secrets are used to securely store sensitive data, such as passwords or access tokens. These resources ensure that configuration management is consistent and centralized, and they prevent sensitive data from being exposed in the container images themselves.

Continuous deployment is another area where Kubernetes enhances the microservices deployment process. With Kubernetes, teams can define declarative deployment configurations, which describe the desired state of the system. These configurations are stored in YAML or JSON files and can be version-controlled alongside application code. Kubernetes continuously monitors the deployed services and ensures that the actual state matches the desired state, automatically correcting any discrepancies. This declarative model allows for efficient management of microservices in production, enabling automated rollbacks, blue-green deployments, and canary releases. By using Kubernetes for continuous deployment, teams can ensure that new versions of microservices are delivered seamlessly and that the system remains stable even as updates are rolled out.

Kubernetes provides a comprehensive suite of tools for managing microservices in a scalable, resilient, and automated way. It simplifies many of the operational challenges that come with running distributed systems, such as service discovery, load balancing, scaling, and fault tolerance. With Kubernetes, microservices teams can focus on developing their services and let the platform handle the complexities of deployment, scaling, and networking. Whether deploying to on-premises infrastructure or to the cloud, Kubernetes enables organizations to manage their microservices architectures efficiently, ensuring that services are always available, scalable, and resilient. As the foundation for many modern cloud-native applications, Kubernetes continues to play a pivotal role in the success of microservices-based systems.

Load Balancing in Microservices Architectures

Load balancing is a crucial component in ensuring the availability, reliability, and scalability of microservices architectures. Microservices systems are typically composed of multiple independent services, each running in its own container or instance, and often across different servers or cloud environments. With the dynamic nature of microservices, where services can scale up or down based on demand, managing traffic distribution becomes essential to maintain optimal performance and ensure that no single service is overwhelmed by too many requests. Load balancing ensures that traffic is efficiently distributed across multiple instances of a service, helping to maintain responsiveness and system stability even during periods of high traffic.

In a traditional monolithic architecture, load balancing might be relatively simple, as all components are usually deployed on a single server or within a small set of servers. However, in microservices, services are decoupled and distributed, meaning that they may run in different locations, environments, and containers. These services communicate with one another via APIs or message queues, and each service may have multiple instances running simultaneously to handle traffic. Load balancing in microservices involves routing client requests or internal service requests to the correct instances of a service, distributing the load to prevent any instance from becoming a bottleneck and ensuring the system remains scalable and responsive.

One of the primary goals of load balancing in microservices is to ensure that all instances of a service receive an appropriate share of the traffic. Microservices often scale horizontally, meaning that new instances of a service are spun up to handle increased demand. As new instances are created, load balancing ensures that traffic is distributed evenly across these instances, improving the system's ability to handle spikes in demand. Without effective load balancing, some instances could be underutilized, while others could be overwhelmed, leading to performance degradation and increased latency.

There are several strategies for load balancing in microservices architectures, each of which is suitable for different use cases. One common approach is round-robin load balancing, where incoming requests are distributed sequentially to each available instance of a service. This approach is simple to implement and works well when the instances are relatively homogeneous and can handle a similar amount of traffic. However, round-robin load balancing does not take into account the current load or performance of each instance, which can lead to inefficiencies if some instances are more resource-intensive or less responsive than others.

Another approach is weighted load balancing, where traffic is distributed based on the capacity or performance of each service instance. In this model, each instance is assigned a weight that reflects its ability to handle traffic. For example, a more powerful instance with more resources might be assigned a higher weight, while a less powerful instance would receive a lower weight. This strategy helps ensure that requests are routed to the most capable instances, improving the efficiency of traffic distribution and preventing underperforming instances from becoming overloaded.

For microservices that require more complex routing, such as those with dependencies on other services or with varying levels of demand across different regions, more sophisticated load balancing algorithms can be used. One such algorithm is least connections load balancing, where traffic is directed to the instance with the fewest active connections. This strategy ensures that no instance is overburdened with long-running connections, which can be particularly useful in systems with variable request durations or unpredictable traffic patterns. Similarly, random load balancing, where requests are distributed randomly across instances, can help to prevent any one instance from being hit with an unexpectedly large volume of traffic.

In microservices systems, load balancing is not limited to external client requests but also applies to internal service-to-service communication. Since microservices often rely on other services to complete their tasks, managing load within the system is just as important as managing load from external clients. Service discovery plays a key role in enabling internal load balancing. Service discovery allows microservices to dynamically register and discover each other, enabling load balancing mechanisms to route requests to the correct service instances. Tools like Consul, Eureka, and Kubernetes are commonly used to implement service discovery and facilitate dynamic load balancing within microservices environments.

Kubernetes, in particular, provides native support for load balancing in microservices architectures. Kubernetes uses a component called a Service to expose a set of pods (containers) as a single entity, ensuring that traffic is evenly distributed among the pods. Kubernetes supports several types of load balancing, including internal load balancing between pods and external load balancing for incoming client traffic. The Kubernetes service automatically updates the load balancer when new instances are added or removed, making it ideal for managing dynamic scaling in microservices environments. Kubernetes also provides automatic health checks, ensuring that traffic is only directed to healthy instances of a service.

Another key aspect of load balancing in microservices is managing stateful services. Many microservices need to maintain state information, such as user sessions or database connections, across multiple requests. Load balancing for stateful services can be more complex because requests from the same client often need to be routed to the same instance to ensure consistency and avoid session loss. Sticky sessions, also known as session affinity, is a load balancing technique that routes requests from the same client to the same service instance. This ensures that clients' requests are handled by the same instance, preserving their session state and preventing issues related to session management. While sticky sessions can be useful for stateful services, they can also create imbalances in traffic distribution, as some instances may become overloaded with requests from clients requiring session persistence.

In microservices architectures, load balancing must also account for fault tolerance and resiliency. Since services are often distributed across multiple nodes and can experience failures, it is important to ensure that load balancing mechanisms can handle service outages or downtime. Failover mechanisms can be incorporated into load balancing to automatically reroute traffic to healthy instances when one or more instances fail. This enhances the resiliency of the system and ensures that the system remains available, even in the event of failures. Load balancing tools like HAProxy and Nginx provide built-in failover capabilities, ensuring that traffic is redirected to healthy instances if a failure is detected.

Monitoring and metrics are also crucial when it comes to load balancing in microservices systems. In order to ensure that load balancing is functioning effectively, it is essential to track the performance of each service instance and the distribution of traffic. Tools like Prometheus and Grafana can be used to collect and visualize metrics on request rates, response times, and resource utilization, helping teams identify potential bottlenecks or issues with load balancing. Monitoring also allows teams to detect imbalances in traffic distribution or instances that are struggling to handle their share of traffic, enabling them to take corrective actions before performance degradation impacts users.

Load balancing plays a critical role in the performance, scalability, and reliability of microservices architectures. By ensuring that traffic is distributed evenly and efficiently across service instances, load balancing helps maintain the responsiveness and availability of the system, even as it scales to handle increased demand. Whether through simple algorithms like round-robin or more complex strategies like least connections and weighted balancing, effective load balancing ensures that microservices can deliver high-quality, consistent experiences to users. With the support of service discovery, container orchestration tools like Kubernetes, and advanced monitoring techniques, teams can ensure that their microservices architectures remain resilient, efficient, and scalable.

Microservices and Cloud Platforms: AWS, Azure, and GCP

Cloud platforms have become integral to the adoption and scaling of microservices architectures. By leveraging the computing power, storage, and managed services offered by cloud providers like Amazon Web Services (AWS), Microsoft Azure, and Google Cloud Platform (GCP), organizations can easily deploy, manage, and scale microservices with minimal overhead. These platforms provide a wide range of tools and services that simplify the management of microservices, ensuring high availability, scalability, and reliability. The cloud environment enhances the flexibility of microservices by offering automated deployment, container orchestration, and robust monitoring solutions, which are essential for modern distributed systems.

AWS, Azure, and GCP are three of the most popular cloud platforms that provide comprehensive support for microservices architectures. Each platform offers unique features and services, but all share the common goal of simplifying the deployment and management of microservices. AWS, for instance, is a pioneer in cloud computing and has an extensive ecosystem of services designed to support microservices. Azure, with its strong integration into enterprise environments and Microsoft technologies, provides a seamless experience for organizations already invested in the Microsoft ecosystem. GCP, known for its focus on data analytics, machine learning, and containerized workloads, has become a preferred choice for organizations focusing on cloud-native applications and big data solutions.

When it comes to microservices, one of the primary concerns is managing the deployment of services and ensuring they can scale effectively. Cloud platforms like AWS, Azure, and GCP provide several tools for container orchestration, the most popular being Kubernetes.

Kubernetes is an open-source platform for automating the deployment, scaling, and management of containerized applications. Each of the major cloud providers offers a managed Kubernetes service, such as Amazon Elastic Kubernetes Service (EKS), Azure Kubernetes Service (AKS), and Google Kubernetes Engine (GKE). These services allow organizations to deploy, manage, and scale microservices in a Kubernetes environment with minimal setup and configuration. Kubernetes enables the automation of service discovery, load balancing, scaling, and rolling updates, making it an essential tool for managing microservices in the cloud.

AWS offers a range of services tailored for microservices architectures. In addition to EKS, AWS provides a suite of other services that are useful for microservices deployments. For example, AWS Lambda allows developers to run serverless microservices that can scale automatically in response to incoming events. This removes the need to manage infrastructure and is ideal for microservices that have unpredictable or variable workloads. Amazon ECS (Elastic Container Service) is another popular service for managing containers on AWS, allowing users to run and scale containerized applications without managing the underlying infrastructure. For storage and databases, AWS provides services like Amazon S3 for object storage, Amazon RDS for relational databases, and Amazon DynamoDB for NoSQL data, which can be easily integrated with microservices to store and retrieve data.

Azure also provides a comprehensive set of tools for building and deploying microservices. Azure Kubernetes Service (AKS) is the primary service for managing containerized applications, and it integrates well with other Azure services like Azure Active Directory for authentication, Azure Monitor for monitoring and logging, and Azure Load Balancer for distributing traffic across services. Azure also offers Azure Functions, a serverless compute service similar to AWS Lambda, which allows organizations to build microservices that are event-driven and scale automatically. For storage, Azure offers a range of services including Azure Blob Storage for object storage, Azure SQL Database for relational data, and Cosmos DB for globally distributed NoSQL storage, which can be easily integrated into a microservices architecture. Azure's integration with Microsoft products like .NET and Windows Server also makes it a preferred choice for organizations that rely on these technologies.

GCP is another powerful platform for deploying and managing microservices. GCP's Google Kubernetes Engine (GKE) is a fully managed service for running Kubernetes clusters in the cloud, and it integrates seamlessly with Google Cloud's ecosystem. GKE allows developers to deploy microservices quickly and scale them efficiently while benefiting from Google's global infrastructure. For serverless microservices, GCP offers Cloud Functions, which automatically scale in response to events without requiring infrastructure management. GCP also provides a range of database and storage options, such as Google Cloud Storage for object storage, Cloud SQL for relational databases, and Cloud Firestore for NoSQL data. Google's data analytics and machine learning services, such as BigQuery and TensorFlow, can also be used in conjunction with microservices for advanced data processing and analysis, which makes GCP particularly attractive for data-driven microservices architectures.

One of the primary benefits of using AWS, Azure, or GCP for microservices is their ability to scale horizontally in response to changing demands. Microservices are often designed to be stateless and loosely coupled, making them ideal candidates for cloud-based infrastructure. With the cloud, services can be easily scaled up or down depending on traffic and load, ensuring optimal performance and resource utilization. Cloud platforms provide automatic scaling features, such as AWS Auto Scaling, Azure Virtual Machine Scale Sets, and GCP's Autoscaler, which monitor traffic and automatically adjust the number of running instances of a service to meet demand. This elastic scaling is one of the key advantages of cloud platforms, enabling microservices systems to handle varying levels of traffic without manual intervention.

In addition to scaling, AWS, Azure, and GCP also offer a range of monitoring and logging tools that are essential for maintaining the health and performance of microservices. Microservices systems often consist of many distributed services, which can make it difficult to track the flow of requests and identify issues. Cloud platforms offer services like AWS CloudWatch, Azure Monitor, and Google Cloud Monitoring, which aggregate logs, metrics, and traces from all services in a centralized location. These tools provide real-time visibility into the performance of microservices, helping teams detect issues, track service health, and optimize system performance. Cloud providers also offer distributed tracing services, such as AWS X-Ray, Azure Application Insights, and Google Cloud Trace, which allow teams to trace requests as they move across multiple services, enabling them to identify performance bottlenecks and service failures.

Security is another critical aspect of microservices in the cloud. AWS, Azure, and GCP offer robust security tools to ensure that microservices are protected against unauthorized access and vulnerabilities. These platforms provide identity and access management services, such as AWS IAM, Azure Active Directory, and Google Cloud Identity, which allow teams to define and enforce access controls for microservices. In addition, cloud providers offer encryption services for data at rest and in transit, ensuring that sensitive data is protected. By using these tools, organizations can implement fine-grained security policies and ensure that their microservices architectures are secure and compliant with industry standards.

Microservices in the cloud offer organizations the flexibility, scalability, and reliability needed to build modern applications. AWS, Azure, and GCP provide the infrastructure, tools, and services required to deploy, manage, and scale microservices, making it easier to build cloud-native applications. Each platform offers unique services and integrations, but all share the ability to automate the deployment and scaling of microservices, manage service dependencies, monitor system health, and ensure security. By leveraging the power of cloud platforms, organizations can streamline their microservices architecture, improving their ability to deliver high-quality, resilient, and scalable applications.

Hybrid Cloud and Microservices Deployment

The concept of a hybrid cloud has gained significant traction in recent years, particularly in the context of microservices deployment. A hybrid cloud environment allows organizations to combine on-premises infrastructure with public cloud resources, creating a more flexible and scalable infrastructure that can meet varying business needs. In a hybrid cloud, an organization can run certain workloads on private infrastructure while utilizing the public cloud for others, creating a balanced approach to data security, compliance, and cost management. When deploying microservices in a hybrid cloud, organizations can benefit from the cloud-native advantages of scalability and flexibility while maintaining control over sensitive data and workloads that need to remain on-premises or within a private cloud. This combination of private and public cloud resources offers a powerful strategy for optimizing the deployment of microservices in a dynamic and evolving IT landscape.

Microservices are a natural fit for cloud environments, as they are designed to be loosely coupled, independently deployable services that can scale dynamically based on demand. When combined with the hybrid cloud approach, microservices allow organizations to leverage the best of both worlds: the flexibility and elasticity of the public cloud, alongside the control and security of on-premises infrastructure. This is particularly valuable for organizations that operate in industries with strict regulatory requirements or have legacy systems that cannot easily be migrated to the cloud. By adopting a hybrid cloud strategy, organizations can continue to utilize their existing on-premises infrastructure while modernizing their application architecture through the use of microservices in the public cloud.

One of the key benefits of hybrid cloud deployment for microservices is the ability to choose where each service should run based on its specific requirements. For example, services that require high performance or have strict data residency requirements can be deployed on private infrastructure, while services that need to scale quickly in response to variable demand can be deployed in the public cloud. The public cloud provides nearly infinite resources, allowing microservices to scale horizontally by adding more instances as needed. This elasticity ensures that organizations can handle spikes in traffic without having to invest in additional physical hardware or worry about resource constraints. Meanwhile, services that handle sensitive data or require low-latency access can run on-premises or in a private cloud, ensuring compliance with data protection regulations while still benefiting from the efficiencies of a microservices architecture.

Hybrid cloud environments also facilitate disaster recovery and business continuity by distributing workloads across multiple locations. In the event of an outage or failure in the private data center, organizations can shift workloads to the public cloud, ensuring that critical services remain operational. Similarly, workloads running in the public cloud can be backed up to a private cloud or on-premises infrastructure, providing an additional layer of protection against data loss or service disruptions. The flexibility of hybrid cloud architectures enables organizations to implement failover strategies and disaster recovery plans that can maintain service availability even in the face of infrastructure failures.

Deploying microservices in a hybrid cloud environment requires effective management of the network and communication between the private and public cloud components. Microservices typically communicate with each other via APIs or message queues, and ensuring seamless communication between services deployed in different environments is crucial for maintaining system performance and reliability. Service mesh technologies, such as Istio or Linkerd, are commonly used in hybrid cloud deployments to manage microservices communication. A service mesh provides a layer of abstraction for managing service-to-service communication, ensuring that services can securely and reliably interact with each other, regardless of whether they are running in the private or public cloud. This helps to simplify the complexity of managing microservices in a hybrid cloud environment, as it abstracts away the underlying network infrastructure and provides tools for load balancing, traffic routing, service discovery, and monitoring.

A critical consideration when deploying microservices in a hybrid cloud is the management of data. Microservices architectures typically involve multiple services that each own their own data store, whether it's a relational database, NoSQL database, or file storage. When these services are distributed across a hybrid cloud, data consistency and synchronization between on-premises and cloud databases must be carefully managed. To address this, organizations may use technologies such as data replication, event-driven architectures, and distributed databases to ensure that data is kept consistent across different environments. Additionally, hybrid cloud solutions often include tools for managing data backups, data synchronization, and disaster recovery, which are essential for maintaining the integrity and availability of data across both public and private clouds.

Security is another key concern when deploying microservices in a hybrid cloud environment. The distribution of services across multiple infrastructures creates potential attack surfaces and increases the complexity of managing security policies. In a hybrid cloud, it is essential to implement robust security measures that protect data in transit, as well as services running in both the public and private cloud environments. Encryption, identity management, and access control mechanisms should be applied consistently across the entire hybrid cloud environment. Tools such as cloud-native firewalls, VPNs, and private networking options can be used to secure communication between on-premises and cloud resources, while identity and access management solutions like AWS IAM, Azure Active Directory, or Google Identity Platform can help manage user and service authentication across environments. Multi-factor authentication, along with role-based access control, should be used to restrict access to sensitive resources, ensuring that only authorized users and services can interact with critical systems.

Hybrid cloud deployments for microservices also require careful management of the CI/CD (Continuous Integration/Continuous Delivery) pipeline. The development, testing, and deployment of microservices in a hybrid cloud environment must account for the distribution of services across both private and public clouds. The CI/CD pipeline needs to ensure that services are built, tested, and deployed correctly, regardless of where they are running. This means integrating tools like Kubernetes, Docker, and Jenkins with both cloud environments to automate the deployment process and ensure that microservices are consistently and reliably deployed across the hybrid cloud. By using automation, organizations can reduce human error, improve consistency, and accelerate the delivery of new features and updates, all while maintaining control over the deployment process.

The management and monitoring of microservices in a hybrid cloud environment are also crucial for maintaining system health and performance. Cloud platforms provide built-in monitoring and logging services, such as AWS CloudWatch, Azure Monitor, and Google Cloud Operations, that can help track the performance of microservices and detect anomalies or failures. However, since services are distributed across different environments, it is important to integrate monitoring solutions that can provide a unified view of the system's health. Distributed tracing tools like Jaeger or Zipkin can be used to track requests as they flow across the hybrid cloud, providing insights into latency, service dependencies, and performance bottlenecks. By using centralized logging and monitoring tools, organizations can gain real-time visibility into the behavior of their microservices, enabling them to quickly detect and resolve issues.

Hybrid cloud deployments offer organizations the flexibility to leverage the benefits of both private and public cloud environments. By adopting microservices in a hybrid cloud, organizations can optimize resource utilization, improve scalability, enhance security, and increase reliability. Whether managing traffic distribution, data synchronization, or service communication, hybrid cloud strategies provide a robust foundation for building and deploying microservices that are both efficient and resilient. Through careful management of infrastructure, security, and CI/CD pipelines, organizations can create a cloud-native microservices environment that supports their evolving business needs while maintaining control and compliance.

Microservices and Serverless Architectures

The rise of serverless architectures has had a profound impact on the way organizations build and deploy applications, particularly in the context of microservices. Serverless computing, sometimes referred to as Function-as-a-Service (FaaS), abstracts away the management of infrastructure, allowing developers to focus purely on writing code while the cloud provider handles the underlying resources. This approach aligns well with microservices because it enables the deployment of small, autonomous functions that perform specific tasks in response to events, allowing for a highly scalable, cost-efficient, and flexible system. The combination of microservices and serverless architectures brings numerous benefits but also introduces unique challenges, requiring organizations to rethink traditional methods of service management, deployment, and scaling.

Microservices architectures, which involve breaking down applications into small, independent services, have become increasingly popular for their ability to improve scalability, flexibility, and maintainability. However, managing these services at scale can be complex and resource-intensive. Traditional microservices deployments often rely on containers or virtual machines, where each service is packaged into an isolated container with its own infrastructure. While this approach works well for many use cases, it can result in wasted resources, especially when services experience variable or unpredictable traffic patterns. Serverless architectures, on the other hand, address this issue by automatically scaling individual functions in response to demand, enabling the deployment of microservices without worrying about provisioning or maintaining infrastructure.

One of the main advantages of using serverless architectures for microservices is the ability to scale automatically. In a serverless environment, functions are triggered by events, such as HTTP requests, database changes, or message queue notifications. As these events occur, the serverless platform automatically provisions the necessary resources to handle the workload, scaling the function up or down based on demand. This eliminates the need for manual intervention or resource allocation, allowing services to scale seamlessly without the overhead of managing servers or containers. For example, if a microservice experiences a sudden spike in traffic, the serverless platform can spin up more instances of the function to handle the increased load, ensuring that the service remains responsive. Conversely, if traffic decreases, the platform can scale down the service, reducing costs by only using resources when they are needed.

Serverless architectures also offer a cost-efficient model for deploying microservices. Traditional deployments often require provisioning a fixed amount of infrastructure, such as virtual machines or containers, to handle peak traffic. This can result in underutilized resources during periods of low demand, leading to wasted costs. In a serverless model, organizations only pay for the compute resources that are actually used, based on the number of function invocations or execution time.

This pay-as-you-go model ensures that organizations are not paying for idle resources, making it an ideal solution for microservices with variable or unpredictable workloads. This cost-efficiency can be particularly beneficial for small and medium-sized businesses, startups, or applications with fluctuating usage patterns, as it allows them to scale without incurring significant upfront infrastructure costs.

Serverless also simplifies the operational overhead associated with running microservices. In traditional deployments, developers and operations teams are responsible for provisioning, managing, and maintaining the underlying infrastructure for each microservice. This involves tasks such as setting up servers, configuring load balancing, scaling services, and ensuring high availability. With serverless, these responsibilities are offloaded to the cloud provider, allowing teams to focus more on writing business logic and less on managing infrastructure. This can significantly speed up development cycles, reduce operational complexity, and allow teams to deliver new features more quickly. Additionally, serverless platforms often provide built-in monitoring, logging, and security features, further reducing the operational burden.

Despite these advantages, there are challenges when using serverless architectures in conjunction with microservices. One of the key challenges is managing the stateless nature of serverless functions. Microservices are often designed to be stateless, meaning that they do not retain any information between invocations. However, serverless functions are inherently stateless as well, which can create difficulties when services need to maintain state information across multiple requests. For example, if a user session needs to be preserved across several interactions with a microservice, a serverless function cannot store that session data directly. Instead, external storage solutions such as databases or distributed caches are required to manage state. This can add complexity to the architecture, as developers must ensure that stateful services are correctly integrated with the stateless functions.

Another challenge with serverless microservices is cold start latency. When a serverless function is invoked after being idle for a period of time, there can be a delay as the platform provisions the necessary resources to execute the function. This is known as a cold start, and while the latency is typically short, it can still be noticeable, especially for high-performance applications or services that require low response times. Cold starts are more common in serverless environments, as functions are designed to scale down to zero when not in use, reducing resource costs. However, in cases where performance is critical, organizations may need to consider techniques to minimize cold start times, such as keeping certain functions "warm" or using provisioned concurrency features provided by cloud platforms.

Another consideration when deploying microservices with serverless architectures is the complexity of orchestration. Serverless functions are often event-driven, meaning that they are triggered by specific events or inputs. However, many microservices workflows require coordination between multiple functions to perform a larger task. Orchestrating these functions can become complex, as each function must be invoked in the correct order, and the system must handle retries, timeouts, and error handling. Tools like AWS Step Functions, Azure Durable Functions, and Google Cloud Workflows provide a way to manage the orchestration of serverless functions, allowing developers to define workflows and handle complex scenarios such as retries, parallel execution, and conditional logic. These tools help to simplify the process of creating workflows from multiple serverless functions, but they still require careful planning to ensure that the architecture is efficient and reliable.

Security is also an important consideration when using serverless architectures for microservices. In traditional server-based architectures, security policies and controls are typically managed at the infrastructure level. However, in a serverless environment, security is handled at the function level, and developers must ensure that each function is properly secured. This includes implementing proper authentication and authorization mechanisms, encrypting data in transit and at rest, and managing API security. Cloud providers offer built-in security features for serverless environments, such as AWS IAM (Identity and Access Management), Azure Active Directory, and Google Cloud IAM, which allow developers to set fine-grained permissions for each function. However, securing serverless microservices requires careful attention to detail, as the distributed and ephemeral nature of serverless functions can introduce new attack vectors.

Serverless architectures are also ideal for event-driven microservices. Many microservices applications rely on asynchronous communication, where services produce events that trigger other services to take action. Serverless functions excel in this type of environment because they can be easily triggered by events from message queues, event streams, or other sources. This event-driven model allows for decoupling of services, where services are triggered by events rather than direct API calls. This reduces the dependencies between services and enhances the scalability and resilience of the system. Serverless platforms like AWS Lambda, Azure Functions, and Google Cloud Functions integrate well with event-driven systems, enabling the development of highly responsive and scalable microservices architectures.

Microservices and serverless architectures complement each other well, offering scalability, flexibility, and cost-efficiency. While serverless computing abstracts much of the infrastructure management, allowing developers to focus on business logic, it also presents challenges such as managing state, handling cold starts, and orchestrating complex workflows. By leveraging serverless platforms in conjunction with event-driven and stateless microservices, organizations can build highly scalable, cost-effective applications. However, careful design and consideration of orchestration, security, and performance are required to fully realize the potential of serverless microservices architectures.

Managing Microservices with Service Mesh

In a microservices architecture, where each service operates independently, communication between services becomes a critical aspect of maintaining the overall system. As the number of services grows, managing the interactions between them can become increasingly complex. This complexity is amplified when considering factors such as service discovery, load balancing, security, and monitoring. A service mesh offers a powerful solution to these challenges by providing a dedicated infrastructure layer that manages service-to-service communication. By abstracting the underlying networking details, a service mesh ensures that microservices can communicate securely, reliably, and efficiently. It also simplifies operational tasks such as monitoring, logging, and tracing, making it easier to manage the growing complexity of microservices environments.

At its core, a service mesh is a set of components that work together to handle the communication between microservices. It typically consists of a data plane and a control plane. The data plane is responsible for handling the actual communication between services, while the control plane manages the configuration and orchestration of the data plane. The data plane is often implemented using lightweight proxies that are deployed alongside each microservice instance. These proxies intercept and manage traffic between services, ensuring that the communication is secure, reliable, and efficient. The control plane provides tools for configuring and monitoring the behavior of the proxies, allowing teams to manage the communication patterns, traffic routing, and security policies across the microservices architecture.

One of the primary advantages of using a service mesh is its ability to manage service discovery. In a microservices architecture, services are frequently deployed and scaled dynamically, which can make it challenging for services to locate one another. Service discovery enables services to automatically detect and connect with other services without requiring manual configuration. A service mesh typically integrates with service discovery mechanisms, allowing the proxies in the data plane to automatically update their routing tables as services are added or removed. This means that services can communicate with each other without needing to know the specific location or instance of the other service, simplifying the process of service-to-service communication and reducing the need for manual intervention.

In addition to service discovery, a service mesh can handle load balancing, ensuring that traffic is distributed efficiently across multiple instances of a service. Load balancing is essential in a microservices architecture, where each service may be replicated to handle high levels of traffic. The proxies in the data plane can distribute incoming requests across available instances of a service, using strategies such as round-robin, least connections, or weighted distribution. This ensures that no single instance is overwhelmed with traffic, improving the overall performance and availability of the system. Service meshes can also implement advanced load balancing features, such as traffic splitting, allowing teams to implement canary releases or blue-green deployments to test new versions of a service with a subset of users.

Security is another critical aspect of microservices communication, and a service mesh can play a key role in securing service-to-service interactions. Microservices often operate in a distributed environment, with services running on different machines, containers, or even in different cloud regions. This distributed nature can make it difficult to ensure secure communication between services. A service mesh provides features such as mutual TLS (Transport Layer Security), which encrypts communication between services and ensures that both the client and server are authenticated before establishing a connection. This prevents man-in-the-middle attacks and ensures that only authorized services can communicate with each other. The service mesh also allows teams to define fine-grained access control policies, ensuring that services can only communicate with other services that they are authorized to interact with.

One of the most powerful features of a service mesh is its ability to provide observability into the communication between microservices. In a distributed system, it can be challenging to understand how services are interacting and where performance bottlenecks or failures are occurring. A service mesh collects telemetry data from the proxies in the data plane, providing detailed insights into the performance of each service and the overall system. This data includes metrics such as request rates, latency, error rates, and service dependencies, as well as distributed traces that allow teams to track the flow of requests across services. By centralizing this data, the service mesh makes it easier to monitor and troubleshoot microservices environments, helping teams detect issues before they impact users and optimize the performance of the system.

In addition to metrics and tracing, a service mesh also enables logging, which is essential for understanding the behavior of services and diagnosing issues. Each proxy in the data plane can capture logs for the requests and responses that pass through it, providing detailed information about the interactions between services. This log data can be integrated with centralized logging systems, such as the ELK stack (Elasticsearch, Logstash, and Kibana) or Fluentd, to provide a unified view of the system's behavior. By collecting and analyzing these logs, teams can quickly identify patterns, such as errors or performance bottlenecks, and take action to resolve them.

Another key feature of a service mesh is its ability to manage traffic routing and resilience. In a microservices architecture, services are often deployed in multiple regions or availability zones to ensure high availability and fault tolerance. A service mesh provides the tools to manage traffic routing between these regions, ensuring that requests are routed to the closest or most available instances of a service. The mesh can also implement resilience features such as retries, timeouts, and circuit breakers, which help to ensure that the system remains available even when individual services or network links fail. By implementing these features at the mesh level, teams can avoid implementing them individually in each microservice, reducing complexity and ensuring consistent behavior across the system.

While service meshes provide powerful features for managing microservices communication, they also introduce some complexity. Implementing a service mesh requires careful planning and integration, as it adds an additional layer of infrastructure to the system. Teams must manage the configuration and deployment of the proxies in the data plane, as well as the orchestration of the control plane components. However, many modern service mesh solutions, such as Istio, Linkerd, and Consul Connect, provide user-friendly interfaces and integrations with popular container orchestration platforms like Kubernetes, making it easier to deploy and manage the service mesh in a microservices environment. These tools also offer robust documentation and community support, helping teams adopt and integrate service meshes into their existing workflows.

Service meshes are becoming an essential tool for managing the complexity of microservices architectures. By providing solutions for service discovery, load balancing, security, observability, and resilience, a service mesh simplifies the management of service-to-service communication in distributed systems. It abstracts away many of the operational challenges associated with microservices, enabling teams to focus on building and deploying business logic. As microservices continue to evolve and scale, service meshes will play a crucial role in ensuring that these systems remain secure, reliable, and efficient. By integrating a service mesh into their architecture, organizations can enhance the performance, security, and observability of their microservices environments, while reducing the complexity of managing distributed communication.

Versioning in Microservices

In microservices architectures, versioning is a critical aspect of ensuring that services can evolve independently without disrupting the overall system. As microservices are designed to be small, independent, and loosely coupled, they are often updated or modified over time to meet changing business needs or technological advancements. However, because different services in a microservices architecture may have dependencies on one another, managing versions effectively becomes crucial. Versioning in microservices addresses the challenge of ensuring that different versions of services can coexist, communicate properly, and allow for seamless updates without breaking existing functionality. This ability to handle service evolution while maintaining compatibility is key to the long-term success of a microservices-based system.

One of the primary reasons versioning is so important in microservices is the need for backward compatibility. In traditional monolithic applications, versioning is often easier to manage because the application is deployed as a single unit, and changes to the system can be handled in a controlled manner. In contrast, microservices involve multiple independent services, each with its own codebase and lifecycle. When one service is updated, it may impact others that rely on it, and maintaining compatibility between different versions of services becomes a challenging task. For example, a new version of a service may introduce changes to its API or data structure, which could break the functionality of other services that rely on the previous version of the service. Effective versioning strategies help manage these issues by allowing teams to introduce new versions of a service without affecting the rest of the system.

There are several strategies for versioning microservices, and the approach chosen depends on the nature of the services and the specific needs of the organization. One common approach is API versioning, where the version of a service is reflected in the API it exposes to other services. This allows developers to introduce new versions of an API while maintaining the ability for clients or other services to interact with the previous version. API versioning can be done in a variety of ways, including through URL path versioning, where the version is specified in the URL path, or through header versioning, where the version is specified in the HTTP request headers. Path versioning is often used when the change in the API is significant, as it clearly distinguishes between different versions of the service. Header versioning, on the other hand, is more subtle and can be used when changes are incremental, allowing clients to interact with the service without changing the URL structure.

Another approach to versioning in microservices is the use of semantic versioning, which is a standardized way of versioning software that conveys meaning about the changes in the version. Semantic versioning follows a specific format, typically in the form of MAJOR.MINOR.PATCH, where each component of the version number indicates the scope and nature of the changes. A change in the MAJOR version indicates a breaking change that is not backward-compatible, while a MINOR version change indicates the addition of functionality in a backward-compatible manner. A PATCH version change refers to bug fixes or minor improvements that do not affect the API. By using semantic versioning, teams can clearly communicate the impact of changes and allow consumers of a service to make informed decisions about when to upgrade to a new version. This is especially important in microservices environments, where services are often interdependent, and understanding the nature of changes can help avoid disruptions in service communication.

While versioning APIs and services is crucial, managing data versioning is just as important in microservices architectures. Since each microservice often manages its own data store, the way that data is structured and stored can change over time as services evolve. When a service's data model changes, it can have cascading effects on other services that rely on that data. To manage this, many organizations implement strategies such as database versioning or schema migration. Database versioning involves tracking changes to the database schema over time, ensuring that updates to the schema are applied in a controlled manner. Schema migration tools, such as Liquibase or Flyway, can be used to manage database versioning by automatically applying changes to the schema as part of the deployment process. This ensures that each service's data store remains consistent with the service's API and avoids issues related to data inconsistencies or version mismatches.

In addition to managing changes in the API and data, it is important to handle backward compatibility when updating microservices. One approach to achieving backward compatibility is through the use of feature toggles. Feature toggles allow teams to introduce new functionality into a service without immediately making it available to users or other services. This enables developers to deploy a new version of a service while keeping the old functionality intact for clients that still rely on it. Once the new functionality has been tested and is ready to be used, the feature toggle can be turned on, making the new functionality available. Feature toggles can help manage versioning by allowing teams to decouple the deployment of a service from its activation, making it easier to manage multiple versions of a service over time.

Another important aspect of versioning in microservices is ensuring that services can be rolled back or updated incrementally. In a microservices architecture, it is common for new versions of services to be deployed gradually to minimize the risk of breaking the system. One strategy for rolling out new versions is blue-green deployment, where two versions of a service (the old and the new) are deployed simultaneously, and traffic is gradually shifted from the old version to the new one. This allows teams to monitor the performance of the new version in production while still maintaining the old version as a fallback in case issues arise. Canary releases are another technique used to deploy new versions incrementally, where a small percentage of traffic is directed to the new version of the service, allowing teams to test its behavior in production before rolling it out to all users.

As microservices evolve, managing versioning becomes increasingly complex, especially as the number of services and their interdependencies grows. Effective versioning strategies are essential for ensuring that services can be updated independently without disrupting the entire system. However, it is also important to establish clear communication and governance processes to track and manage versions across the architecture. Tools like version control systems (such as Git), CI/CD pipelines, and automated testing frameworks can help manage the complexity of versioning by providing a centralized way to track changes, automate deployments, and validate the behavior of services at different versions.

Versioning in microservices is a key part of managing the lifecycle of a distributed system. It allows teams to introduce changes and new functionality without breaking existing services, ensuring that the system remains stable and reliable even as it evolves. Whether through API versioning, semantic versioning, or database versioning, organizations must carefully manage the updates and changes to their microservices to ensure that services can scale, adapt, and remain interoperable. Effective versioning helps prevent disruptions, improves communication between teams, and provides the flexibility needed to evolve microservices architectures in a controlled and predictable manner.

Rolling Updates and Continuous Delivery for Microservices

In a microservices architecture, the ability to deploy changes quickly and reliably is essential to maintaining a fast-paced development lifecycle and ensuring the system remains responsive to business needs. Rolling updates, in conjunction with continuous delivery (CD), provide an effective way to deploy new versions of microservices without causing downtime or service disruption. These techniques enable teams to update individual services incrementally, reducing the risk of failure and ensuring that the system can continue to function even as new features or bug fixes are introduced. The combination of rolling updates and continuous delivery has become a cornerstone of modern software deployment strategies, helping organizations maintain high availability, flexibility, and reliability while keeping up with the rapid pace of change in microservices environments.

Rolling updates are a deployment strategy that enables organizations to update microservices incrementally, one step at a time, without taking the entire system offline. The goal of a rolling update is to replace old instances of a service with new ones in a controlled and gradual manner, allowing the system to remain fully functional throughout the process. In a microservices architecture, services are often deployed in clusters or distributed environments, with multiple instances of the same service running to handle traffic and ensure high availability. During a rolling update, new instances of a service are deployed alongside the old ones, and traffic is gradually shifted to the new instances as they come online. This allows the update process to be smooth and avoids the need for a system-wide shutdown, which could lead to downtime and affect user experience.

The key advantage of rolling updates is that they allow for minimal disruption to the system. Since the update occurs incrementally, only a small portion of the system is affected at any given time. This reduces the risk of introducing issues that could affect the entire system, as the impact is contained to a limited set of services or instances. Additionally, rolling updates provide an opportunity for teams to monitor the system's performance during the deployment process. If any issues arise, teams can stop the update and roll back to the previous version, ensuring that the system remains stable and operational. This ability to test and monitor the new version before fully rolling it out to all instances is particularly valuable in microservices environments, where different services may have complex interdependencies.

For rolling updates to be effective, the system needs to be designed with high availability and fault tolerance in mind. In a microservices architecture, services are typically stateless, meaning they do not store any session or state information locally. This makes it easier to replace instances of a service without affecting its functionality, as requests can be routed to other available instances. However, services that maintain state or require persistence, such as databases or cache layers, present additional challenges during rolling updates. These services must be carefully managed to ensure that data consistency is maintained while new versions are deployed. Techniques such as database schema migration, data versioning, and the use of feature toggles can help ensure that stateful services are updated in a way that does not disrupt the rest of the system.

Continuous delivery plays a crucial role in enabling rolling updates for microservices. CD is a software development practice that automates the process of building, testing, and deploying code changes to production. By integrating continuous integration (CI) and continuous delivery pipelines, teams can automatically deploy new versions of microservices as soon as they pass automated tests, ensuring that updates are delivered quickly and consistently. Continuous delivery removes much of the manual overhead associated with deploying changes, allowing teams to release new features, bug fixes, or security patches more frequently without sacrificing quality or reliability.

In a microservices environment, continuous delivery ensures that each service can be deployed independently without affecting the rest of the system. Since microservices are loosely coupled and communicate with each other through well-defined APIs, teams can deploy updates to individual services without needing to coordinate changes across the entire system. This decoupling allows teams to deploy and update services on their own schedule, reducing the time it takes to deliver new functionality to users. By using automated testing and deployment tools, continuous delivery also ensures that changes are validated at every stage of the development pipeline, minimizing the risk of introducing bugs or regressions into the system.

One of the challenges in implementing continuous delivery in a microservices architecture is managing service dependencies. Microservices often rely on each other to complete business processes, and changes to one service can impact others. For example, a change in the API of one service might break functionality in other services that depend on it. To mitigate this risk, teams can use versioning strategies and backward compatibility techniques to ensure that services can evolve independently while still maintaining compatibility with one another. Additionally, teams can use canary releases or blue-green deployments to test new versions of services with a subset of users before fully rolling them out, providing an additional layer of safety during the deployment process.

Automating the deployment process is essential for implementing continuous delivery and rolling updates effectively. Tools such as Jenkins, GitLab CI, and CircleCI can be used to create and manage CI/CD pipelines, automating the entire process from code commit to production deployment. These tools integrate with version control systems like Git, ensuring that each change is automatically built, tested, and deployed in a consistent and repeatable manner. The pipeline can include steps for running unit tests, integration tests, and security checks, ensuring that only high-quality code is deployed to production. Once the code passes all tests, the pipeline can trigger the deployment process, starting a rolling update for the affected services.

Another important aspect of rolling updates and continuous delivery in microservices is monitoring and observability. As services are updated incrementally, it is crucial to track their performance and ensure that they are functioning correctly. Tools like Prometheus, Grafana, and Datadog can be used to collect and visualize metrics such as response times, error rates, and resource utilization. Distributed tracing tools like Jaeger or Zipkin allow teams to track the flow of requests across multiple services, helping to identify bottlenecks or failures in the system. By monitoring the system during a rolling update, teams can quickly detect issues and take corrective actions before they affect the end-user experience. This level of visibility is essential for maintaining the stability and performance of the system as it evolves.

One of the primary goals of rolling updates and continuous delivery is to enable faster iteration and innovation without compromising the reliability of the system. In a microservices architecture, this is particularly important, as services are constantly evolving to meet changing business requirements and technological advancements. By using rolling updates and CD, teams can deliver new features, fix bugs, and address security vulnerabilities in a controlled and predictable manner, ensuring that the system remains stable while continuing to grow and improve. These practices help organizations remain agile and responsive to customer needs, allowing them to maintain a competitive edge in a rapidly changing market.

Rolling updates and continuous delivery are integral to the success of microservices architectures, enabling teams to deploy changes quickly, reliably, and with minimal disruption. By using these strategies, organizations can ensure that their microservices systems remain available, scalable, and efficient while allowing for rapid innovation and improvement. Automated deployment pipelines, service versioning, and robust monitoring tools all play a role in making rolling updates and continuous delivery effective in a microservices environment, ensuring that each service can evolve independently while maintaining compatibility and stability across the system. These practices are key to achieving the flexibility, resilience, and responsiveness that modern microservices architectures demand.

Handling State in Stateless Microservices

Microservices are designed to be lightweight, independent, and scalable, offering a solution to the complexity of monolithic applications. One of the key principles of microservices is that they should be stateless, meaning that they do not retain any information about past interactions or transactions. This makes microservices more flexible and scalable, as they can be easily deployed, replaced, or scaled independently without worrying about maintaining state. However, while statelessness is a core tenet of microservices architecture, it introduces significant challenges when it comes to handling state, especially in use cases that require persisting data, tracking user sessions, or maintaining business context over time. Thus, finding efficient and scalable ways to handle state in a stateless architecture is crucial for ensuring the overall functionality of microservices-based systems.

In traditional application architectures, managing state is relatively straightforward. For example, monolithic applications typically store state within a centralized database, allowing the application to retain information about user sessions, preferences, or transaction histories. In contrast, in microservices, each service is intended to be autonomous and stateless. This means that any state information must be handled separately, outside of the service itself. Since the microservice may be deployed on different instances or containers over time, it is critical that it does not rely on local memory or internal data storage. Instead, the state must be managed using external systems, which can be both scalable and resilient.

To handle state in stateless microservices, the most common approach is to use external storage systems such as databases, object stores, or distributed caches. These systems allow microservices to offload state management, ensuring that even as individual instances of services come and go, the state remains intact and accessible. One of the simplest and most widely used forms of state management is through databases. Each microservice typically has its own database or data store, ensuring that it can manage its data independently of other services. These databases may be relational or NoSQL, depending on the nature of the data and the requirements of the service.

For state that needs to persist across multiple service calls or across multiple microservices, distributed data stores are often used. For example, a distributed cache such as Redis or Memcached can be used to store session data or frequently accessed information that needs to be shared across multiple services. These systems allow microservices to quickly retrieve and update state, reducing the load on backend databases and ensuring high performance. However, while distributed caches are highly efficient, they introduce the complexity of ensuring consistency across different instances of a service and ensuring that the data is updated correctly in real-time.

In some use cases, the state of a microservice may need to be shared across multiple microservices or between the front-end and back-end services. In such scenarios, event-driven architectures can be employed to handle state across the system. With an event-driven architecture, state changes in one service can trigger events that other services listen for and respond to. For example, when a customer makes a purchase in an e-commerce system, the order service might generate an event indicating that a new order has been placed. Other services, such as inventory or shipping, can listen for this event and update their own state accordingly. This approach decouples the microservices, ensuring that each service can evolve independently while still maintaining the necessary state across the system. Event-driven systems are typically implemented using message brokers such as Kafka, RabbitMQ, or AWS SNS/SQS, which provide a reliable and scalable means of transmitting state changes between services.

Another challenge in handling state in stateless microservices is managing user sessions. In many applications, users need to be authenticated and their session state must be maintained across multiple interactions. A stateless microservice cannot directly store session information, as it does not retain state between requests. To handle this, session data is typically stored in an external system such as a session store or a distributed cache. For example, a service might use a token-based authentication system such as JSON Web Tokens (JWT), where the user's session state is encoded within the token itself. When the user makes a request to a service, the token is passed along, and the service can decode it to retrieve the session information, without needing to store any state locally. This approach allows the system to remain stateless while still providing a mechanism to track user sessions.

For applications that require complex, long-running workflows, state can also be managed through orchestrated state machines or saga patterns. The saga pattern is commonly used in microservices architectures to manage long-running transactions and workflows that span multiple services. A saga divides a large transaction into smaller, manageable steps, each executed by a separate microservice. Each step in the saga may produce or change state, but the overall system remains stateless because the state is not stored within the individual services. Instead, the state of the entire workflow is managed through events or coordination with a centralized saga orchestrator. This allows microservices to handle complex business logic while maintaining the benefits of statelessness.

One of the advantages of using event-driven architectures, distributed caches, and external databases to handle state is that it helps to maintain the scalability of the system. In a stateless microservices architecture, services can be scaled up or down independently, and new instances can be added without worrying about syncing local state. This flexibility makes it easier to manage the increased demand for services, as resources can be allocated dynamically based on traffic or usage patterns. Furthermore, since the state is external to the service, the failure or removal of a service instance does not result in the loss of state information, ensuring high availability and resilience.

However, handling state in stateless microservices also requires careful consideration of data consistency and transaction management. Since state is distributed across multiple systems, ensuring that the state remains consistent across all services and data stores becomes challenging, particularly when dealing with failures or network partitions. One way to address this is through eventual consistency, a pattern commonly used in distributed systems. Eventual consistency allows the system to reach a consistent state over time, but not necessarily immediately. In situations where immediate consistency is not critical, eventual consistency provides a reliable way to ensure that all parts of the system eventually converge on the same state. Techniques such as distributed transactions, compensation actions, and state reconciliation can be employed to ensure that the system remains consistent even in the face of failures.

Managing state in stateless microservices requires a careful balance between ensuring performance, availability, and consistency. By leveraging external systems such as distributed caches, event-driven architectures, and specialized state management patterns like sagas, organizations can build scalable, resilient systems that maintain the benefits of statelessness while still meeting the need to persist and manage state. As microservices continue to evolve, the tools and strategies for handling state in stateless environments will also advance, enabling organizations to build even more flexible, efficient, and robust applications.

Microservices and Event Sourcing

Event sourcing is a powerful architectural pattern that has gained significant popularity in the context of microservices architectures. It revolves around the concept of storing the state of an application as a sequence of events, rather than storing the current state directly. Each event represents a change or action within the system, capturing the state transition over time. This approach contrasts with traditional methods, where data is stored in a relational database, and the most recent state is retrieved on demand. In microservices, event sourcing provides a robust way to maintain consistency, improve scalability, and ensure that every state transition is auditable and traceable.

In a typical microservices architecture, services often need to maintain their own data stores, resulting in the challenge of ensuring consistency across services. One of the inherent complexities of microservices is managing distributed transactions, where multiple services may need to collaborate to achieve a common goal. Traditional approaches to handling state, such as using databases with immediate consistency, can become problematic when dealing with distributed systems. Event sourcing helps to solve this issue by treating changes as a series of events rather than updating the state directly, enabling a more flexible and decoupled approach to managing service state across distributed services.

The main principle behind event sourcing is that the system's state is rebuilt by replaying a sequence of events. Each event captures a state transition, and the events are stored in an event store, which acts as the central source of truth. This means that instead of simply storing the current state of a service, all the actions that led to that state are preserved. In this way, the system maintains an immutable record of events, providing a full history of all changes that have occurred. When a service needs to access its current state, it can do so by replaying the stored events in the correct order, reconstructing the state from the event stream. This makes event sourcing particularly useful in applications that require strong auditability or need to maintain a history of changes for compliance or debugging purposes.

One of the key advantages of event sourcing in a microservices context is its ability to support eventual consistency. Since each service maintains its own event store, it can independently process and replay events to update its state. This allows for services to operate in isolation without requiring tight coupling to other services, reducing the complexity of managing distributed transactions. Instead of immediately synchronizing data across services, each service updates its state by processing the events relevant to it. Over time, the services will eventually reach a consistent state, even if there are temporary discrepancies due to network delays or failures. This concept of eventual consistency is particularly well-suited to microservices, where services are distributed and may not always be able to synchronize data in real-time.

Event sourcing also provides significant benefits in terms of scalability and performance. Traditional databases often face performance challenges as the size of the data grows, especially when handling complex queries or large volumes of transactions. Event stores, on the other hand, are designed to handle high write throughput, as each new event is simply appended to the event stream, rather than requiring expensive updates to a database. As a result, event sourcing enables services to scale more efficiently by providing fast, append-only writes and avoiding the bottlenecks that can occur in traditional data stores. Moreover, since the events are stored in chronological order, retrieving past state transitions is straightforward, allowing for more efficient querying and data retrieval.

In microservices, event sourcing is often used in combination with other patterns like CQRS (Command Query Responsibility Segregation). CQRS is an architectural pattern that separates the handling of commands (which change the state) from the handling of queries (which read the state). This separation allows for optimization of both read and write operations, as the read model can be tailored for efficient queries, while the write model can focus on capturing and persisting events. In the context of event sourcing, CQRS provides a way to maintain different views of the data, enabling services to handle specific queries without needing to process the full event stream. By using event sourcing with CQRS, microservices can optimize both the performance and scalability of their systems, ensuring that they can handle large volumes of transactions while also providing quick access to relevant data.

Event sourcing also offers benefits in terms of fault tolerance and recovery. Since the system's state is stored as a series of immutable events, recovering from failures becomes a much simpler process. If a service crashes or experiences an issue, it can simply replay the events in its event store to rebuild its state. This makes it possible to recover from failures without needing complex backup or replication strategies. Additionally, since the events themselves are the source of truth, there is no need to worry about data corruption or loss, as the events can be reprocessed from the event store to restore the system to its previous state.

However, event sourcing does come with its own set of challenges, particularly in terms of complexity and managing event schemas. Since events are stored as the primary record of state changes, it is crucial that the events are designed in a way that accurately reflects the business logic and state transitions. This can require careful planning and versioning of event schemas, as changes to the structure of events can affect the ability to replay historical events correctly. Additionally, managing and processing large volumes of events can be complex, especially as the number of services and events grows over time. Event replay and the need to ensure that services can process events in the correct order can also introduce latency, as the service must replay all relevant events to reach the desired state.

To mitigate these challenges, organizations may need to implement strategies for managing event schemas, such as versioning events or using event replay mechanisms that allow older events to be transformed or migrated as necessary. Another important consideration is ensuring that the event store itself is scalable and reliable, as it becomes the central point of truth for the system. Cloud-native event storage solutions like Apache Kafka, Amazon Kinesis, or event streaming platforms can be used to store and process events at scale, providing the necessary performance and reliability to support event sourcing at an enterprise level.

Event sourcing also plays a critical role in ensuring data consistency across distributed services in microservices architectures. Since each microservice can independently process and store its own events, it can maintain consistency within its own boundaries, while still relying on the event stream to synchronize with other services. This decouples services and reduces the need for complex coordination, allowing them to evolve independently while maintaining a shared source of truth. Moreover, event-driven systems can react to business events in real-time, enabling microservices to respond quickly to changes and triggering appropriate actions in other services when necessary.

Event sourcing in microservices is a powerful and flexible pattern that helps organizations manage complexity, scalability, and consistency. By capturing state transitions as a series of events, microservices can maintain a rich history of state changes, support eventual consistency, and improve fault tolerance. While the pattern does introduce challenges around event schema management and service coordination, its benefits in scalability, performance, and maintainability make it a compelling choice for modern distributed systems. Event sourcing, particularly when combined with patterns like CQRS, provides the tools necessary to build scalable, resilient, and performant microservices architectures that can adapt to changing business needs over time.

CQRS (Command Query Responsibility Segregation) and Microservices

Command Query Responsibility Segregation (CQRS) is an architectural pattern that divides the handling of data into two distinct models: commands and queries. Commands represent actions that modify the state of the system, such as creating, updating, or deleting data, while queries are operations that retrieve data without modifying it. This separation allows each model to be optimized independently, leading to more efficient and scalable systems, particularly in complex applications like microservices architectures. Microservices, by design, are distributed, independent services that communicate through well-defined APIs. As microservices architectures grow, managing complex business logic, ensuring performance, and maintaining scalability can become challenging. Implementing CQRS in microservices helps address these concerns by improving the handling of read and write operations and enhancing the system's overall flexibility and responsiveness.

The traditional approach to handling data in applications often involves a single data model that serves both reads and writes. While this model works for smaller applications, it can become inefficient as the system scales, especially in environments like microservices where the load and performance requirements can vary greatly between read and write operations. In a microservices architecture, different services often manage different aspects of the business logic, and each service may have its own database or data store. These services must interact with one another, sometimes in real-time, to process data and handle various operations. As the number of services increases, the need to handle complex queries and commands efficiently becomes more pronounced.

CQRS solves this problem by splitting the responsibilities of data access into two separate models: the command model and the query model. The command model is responsible for modifying the state of the system, while the query model is optimized for retrieving data. By separating the two, each model can be designed to perform its respective task more efficiently. For example, write-heavy services that handle commands can be optimized for high transaction volumes, ensuring that changes to the system are processed quickly. On the other hand, services that handle queries can be optimized for fast data retrieval, using read-optimized data stores such as denormalized databases, caches, or search engines like Elasticsearch. This separation allows microservices to scale independently based on the differing demands of read and write operations.

One of the key advantages of using CQRS in microservices is that it allows for greater flexibility and scalability. By decoupling the command and query responsibilities, organizations can scale each part of the system independently. For example, if the system experiences a surge in read traffic but the write operations remain constant, the query side of the system can be scaled horizontally to accommodate the increased demand. This makes it easier to optimize resource allocation, improve performance, and handle varying workloads without unnecessary overhead. Similarly, since each model operates independently, it's easier to adapt the architecture to meet changing requirements over time, such as implementing new features or integrating with external systems.

Implementing CQRS in microservices also simplifies the development of complex business logic. In traditional architectures, handling both read and write operations in the same model often leads to complex, intertwined code that can be difficult to maintain and scale. By separating the command and query responsibilities, CQRS enables developers to focus on the specific requirements of each part of the system. This results in cleaner, more maintainable code, as each model can be optimized and modified independently. The read model can evolve to meet the needs of the application's users, while the command model can be adapted to handle complex business processes and workflows without affecting the way data is read from the system.

However, the separation of command and query models introduces certain complexities, particularly when it comes to maintaining consistency between the two models. Since the command model modifies the state of the system, and the query model retrieves data, ensuring that both models are kept in sync can be challenging, especially in distributed systems like microservices. This is where event sourcing, a related pattern, comes into play. Event sourcing involves persisting the state of the system as a series of events, rather than directly storing the current state in a database. With event sourcing, the command model generates events that represent state changes, and these events are then propagated to the query model. The query model can rebuild its state by replaying the events, ensuring that it remains consistent with the command model.

In a microservices architecture, event sourcing and CQRS work together to provide a robust solution for managing state and ensuring consistency. Since the event store serves as the single source of truth, all services in the system can subscribe to events and update their state accordingly. This ensures that each service maintains an accurate and up-to-date view of the system's data, while the command and query models remain decoupled. By using this approach, microservices can achieve eventual consistency, where the system as a whole remains in a consistent state over time, even if individual services may be temporarily out of sync.

Another challenge of implementing CQRS in microservices is managing the complexity of data replication. Since the query model often uses a separate database optimized for read operations, the data must be replicated from the command model to the query model. This replication can introduce latency, especially if the data is frequently updated. To address this, microservices often use techniques such as asynchronous messaging or event-driven architectures to propagate changes from the command model to the query model. By using message brokers like Kafka or RabbitMQ, events representing state changes can be sent to the appropriate services, allowing them to update their read models without waiting for immediate synchronization. This ensures that the system remains responsive even in high-volume environments.

While CQRS offers significant benefits in terms of scalability and performance, it also introduces additional infrastructure and operational complexity. Managing multiple data models and ensuring that the command and query models remain in sync requires careful planning and monitoring. It also requires sophisticated tooling for handling event sourcing, messaging, and data replication. Tools like Kubernetes, Docker, and CI/CD pipelines can help automate and manage the deployment and scaling of CQRS-based microservices, making it easier to manage the added complexity. Additionally, logging, monitoring, and tracing tools such as Prometheus, Grafana, and Jaeger can help teams track the behavior of the system, detect performance bottlenecks, and resolve issues quickly.

The implementation of CQRS in a microservices architecture is a powerful way to address the challenges of scaling, performance, and maintainability in complex systems. By separating the command and query responsibilities, microservices can be optimized independently for both read and write operations, allowing the system to scale more efficiently. However, CQRS also introduces challenges in terms of ensuring consistency and managing the complexity of data replication. By combining CQRS with event sourcing and event-driven architectures, organizations can achieve eventual consistency and ensure that their microservices systems remain scalable, reliable, and performant.

Building Fault-Tolerant Microservices with Circuit Breakers

In the world of microservices, fault tolerance is crucial for maintaining system reliability, availability, and user satisfaction. Microservices architectures often involve multiple distributed services communicating with each other, and as the number of services grows, the likelihood of failures increases. A failure in one service can cascade across the system, affecting other services and causing widespread outages. To mitigate this risk, it is essential to design microservices systems with fault tolerance in mind. One of the most effective ways to ensure fault tolerance in microservices is by using circuit breakers. The circuit breaker pattern is a robust solution for detecting failures and preventing them from escalating, allowing the system to remain operational even in the face of service disruptions.

The circuit breaker pattern is inspired by the concept of an electrical circuit breaker, which automatically shuts off power to prevent damage to the system when there is a fault. In a similar way, a circuit breaker in software systems monitors service calls and intervenes when it detects a failure. If a service is repeatedly failing, the circuit breaker "opens" and stops further calls to the failing service, allowing the system to recover. This prevents the system from overloading the failing service and helps maintain the overall system's stability. When the circuit breaker detects that the service has recovered and is functioning properly, it "closes" again, allowing normal communication to resume. This simple yet effective mechanism enables the system to gracefully handle failures and prevent cascading issues from bringing down the entire architecture.

The circuit breaker pattern works by monitoring the health of service calls. When a service is functioning normally, requests pass through the circuit breaker without any interruptions. However, when the failure rate of a service exceeds a predefined threshold, the circuit breaker opens, and further requests are immediately rejected, preventing the system from overwhelming the service with additional calls. This gives the failing service time to recover, without exacerbating the problem by repeatedly attempting to access it. The circuit breaker pattern can be implemented in various stages, such as the closed, open, and half-open states. When the circuit breaker is closed, all requests flow through to the service as usual. When the circuit breaker opens, requests are blocked, and the system takes appropriate actions, such as returning an error response or invoking a fallback mechanism. In the half-open state, the circuit breaker allows a limited number of requests to pass through to determine if the service has recovered.

One of the primary benefits of using circuit breakers in microservices is that they enhance system resilience and prevent service failures from causing widespread outages. Microservices systems are often highly distributed, and a failure in one service can propagate across other services that rely on it. Without circuit breakers, these cascading failures can result in a complete system breakdown. Circuit breakers help isolate failures, ensuring that they do not affect other services and that the system can continue to function, even when some parts of it are unavailable. For example, if a payment service is experiencing high latency or failure, the circuit breaker can prevent the service from being called repeatedly by other services, giving the payment service time to recover without overwhelming it. This improves the overall reliability of the system, ensuring that users continue to have access to the functionality that remains operational.

In addition to enhancing fault tolerance, circuit breakers can help improve system performance. When a service is overwhelmed with requests and unable to handle the load, it can become increasingly slow and unresponsive. By using a circuit breaker to stop further requests from being sent to the failing service, the system can prevent unnecessary strain on the service, allowing it to recover more quickly. This also prevents the system from experiencing the cascading effects of a service failure, which could lead to performance degradation across the entire application. With a circuit breaker in place, microservices can more effectively manage their resources, ensuring that the system as a whole remains responsive, even in the event of service disruptions.

Another important aspect of using circuit breakers in microservices is the ability to provide fallbacks when services fail. When the circuit breaker opens, requests to the failing service can be redirected to a fallback mechanism, such as a cached response, a default value, or an alternative service. This ensures that users are not left with an error message or empty response, improving the user experience even when a service is unavailable. For example, if an inventory service is down, a fallback could return the last known inventory data, allowing users to continue browsing products without experiencing an interruption. This fallback mechanism helps to maintain the functionality of the application and ensures that users can still interact with the system, even when certain parts of it are not fully operational.

While circuit breakers are an essential tool for building fault-tolerant microservices, they must be carefully configured and managed to ensure their effectiveness. Setting appropriate thresholds for failure detection, such as the maximum number of failed requests or the time window for monitoring, is crucial for preventing unnecessary circuit breaker trips. Too sensitive a configuration can result in circuit breakers opening too frequently, causing unnecessary disruption to the system, while too lenient a configuration can lead to failures going undetected, allowing them to escalate. Proper configuration and tuning are essential for balancing resilience with system availability. Additionally, teams must monitor the behavior of circuit breakers in real-time to ensure that they are operating correctly and that the thresholds are still appropriate as the system evolves.

Another consideration when implementing circuit breakers in microservices is ensuring that they are integrated into the broader system monitoring and observability framework. To make informed decisions about when to open or close the circuit breaker, it is important to have real-time visibility into service performance and failure rates. Tools like Prometheus, Grafana, and Jaeger can be used to track the health of services and visualize metrics such as response times, error rates, and failure counts. By integrating circuit breakers with monitoring systems, organizations can gain a deeper understanding of how their services are performing and make data-driven decisions about when to adjust the thresholds or take other corrective actions.

In microservices architectures, communication between services is typically handled via APIs or message queues. Circuit breakers are particularly effective in this context, as they can be implemented at the API level or within the messaging infrastructure. API gateways, for instance, can implement circuit breakers to manage traffic between services, ensuring that requests are automatically routed around failing services. Similarly, message brokers such as Kafka or RabbitMQ can include circuit breaker functionality to prevent message overloads or failures in the message processing pipeline. This provides an additional layer of fault tolerance within the communication layer, ensuring that microservices can continue to communicate even in the presence of failures.

Circuit breakers are an indispensable pattern for building fault-tolerant microservices. They provide a mechanism for isolating failures, preventing cascading issues, and maintaining system stability during service disruptions. By enhancing resilience, improving performance, and offering fallback mechanisms, circuit breakers ensure that microservices systems can remain operational even in the face of challenges. While implementing and managing circuit breakers requires careful configuration and integration with monitoring systems, the benefits they provide in terms of fault tolerance and system reliability are invaluable. As microservices architectures continue to grow in complexity, the use of circuit breakers will remain a key strategy for ensuring that applications are resilient, scalable, and capable of handling failures gracefully.

Observability in Microservices: Metrics, Logs, and Tracing

As microservices architectures grow in complexity, ensuring that the system remains reliable and performant becomes increasingly difficult. Microservices involve many independently deployable services that interact with each other across a distributed environment. As the number of services increases, so does the complexity of managing, monitoring, and troubleshooting the system. Observability, which encompasses metrics, logs, and tracing, plays a vital role in enabling teams to gain visibility into their microservices environments and ensure the system is functioning as expected. It provides the tools and insights needed to monitor the health of services, detect performance bottlenecks, troubleshoot issues, and optimize the overall system.

Metrics are a crucial component of observability, providing quantitative data that helps teams understand the performance and behavior of microservices over time. Metrics capture key performance indicators (KPIs) such as response times, request rates, error rates, and resource utilization, allowing teams to track the health of individual services and the system as a whole. For example, by tracking the average response time of a service, teams can quickly identify performance degradation or slowdowns in the system. Similarly, monitoring error rates can help detect failing services or issues with communication between microservices. Metrics can be collected at various levels, including the service level, API level, or infrastructure level, and can be aggregated into dashboards for real-time monitoring.

The use of metrics also allows teams to set up automated alerts. When a metric exceeds a predefined threshold, such as an increase in error rate or a spike in response time, an alert is triggered to notify the team that something is wrong. This proactive approach to monitoring allows teams to quickly respond to issues before they escalate into system-wide failures. For instance, if the response time of a service exceeds a certain threshold, an alert can be triggered to indicate that the service is experiencing high latency. This allows the team to investigate and resolve the issue before it affects end-users or other services. By leveraging metrics, teams can gain deep insights into the performance of their microservices and react quickly to changing conditions in the system.

Logs provide another critical aspect of observability in microservices. While metrics offer high-level, quantitative insights into the performance of a system, logs provide detailed, context-rich information about individual events and operations. A log is typically a record of events that happen within a service or application, capturing information about the request, response, and any errors or exceptions that occur during processing. Logs are essential for understanding what is happening at the microservice level and for diagnosing issues that cannot be captured by metrics alone. For example, logs may provide detailed information about the failure of a specific operation, such as a database query failure, a missing dependency, or a network timeout, which can help pinpoint the root cause of an issue.

In microservices architectures, logs are particularly important because they provide visibility into the interactions between services. Since microservices are often distributed across multiple nodes or containers, it is essential to track the flow of requests and responses between services. Centralized logging is a common practice in microservices environments, where logs from all services are aggregated into a single location, such as a logging platform like ELK (Elasticsearch, Logstash, Kibana), Fluentd, or Splunk. This makes it easier for teams to search, analyze, and correlate logs across services, enabling them to understand the full context of an issue and troubleshoot more effectively. Centralized logging platforms often provide powerful querying and filtering capabilities, allowing teams to quickly identify patterns, errors, or anomalies in the logs.

One of the challenges of working with logs in microservices is managing the volume of log data. Since each service generates its own logs, the number of logs produced can be substantial, especially in large-scale systems with high traffic. Therefore, it is important to implement log management strategies, such as log rotation, log aggregation, and log filtering, to ensure that logs are stored efficiently and are easily accessible for analysis. By applying appropriate log levels (e.g., debug, info, warning, error), teams can control the verbosity of logs and ensure that only the necessary information is captured for troubleshooting. Additionally, it is essential to ensure that logs contain relevant context, such as unique request IDs or service names, to make it easier to trace the flow of requests and diagnose issues across the system.

Tracing, the third key component of observability, provides a detailed view of the interactions and dependencies between services in a microservices architecture. Tracing allows teams to follow a request as it travels through different services, enabling them to understand how services collaborate and where delays or failures occur. Distributed tracing is a technique that tracks a single request across multiple services, providing a visual representation of the request's journey and helping teams identify bottlenecks, failures, or performance issues. Tools like Jaeger, Zipkin, and OpenTelemetry are commonly used for distributed tracing, offering features to collect, store, and visualize trace data.

In a distributed system, requests often span multiple services, each of which can introduce its own latency. Distributed tracing allows teams to visualize the end-to-end journey of a request, from the initial service to the final response. Each service involved in processing the request generates a "span," which represents a unit of work performed by that service. These spans are linked together by a unique trace ID, allowing the team to trace the path of the request across multiple services and identify the time spent in each service. This detailed insight into the request flow helps teams identify performance bottlenecks, such as slow database queries, inefficient code, or network latency, and optimize the system accordingly.

Tracing is particularly valuable for understanding the interactions between microservices and diagnosing complex issues in distributed systems. Unlike traditional monolithic applications, where the entire system runs in a single process, microservices communicate over networks, making it difficult to track the flow of requests. Tracing provides a solution to this problem by giving teams a clear picture of how services interact and where failures or delays occur. This is especially important for troubleshooting, as it helps teams pinpoint the exact service or step in the process that is causing issues. Additionally, by visualizing the flow of requests and the dependencies between services, tracing allows teams to better understand the architecture of the system and make informed decisions about scaling, optimization, and service decoupling.

Together, metrics, logs, and tracing form the foundation of observability in microservices architectures. These three components provide complementary insights into the performance, behavior, and health of the system, allowing teams to proactively monitor and troubleshoot microservices at scale. Metrics provide high-level quantitative data that helps teams track performance and detect issues, logs offer detailed context-rich information about individual events and errors, and tracing enables teams to visualize the end-to-end flow of requests across services. By integrating these observability tools into the development lifecycle, organizations can build more resilient, efficient, and reliable microservices systems, ensuring that they can quickly detect and resolve issues while delivering a seamless user experience.

Integrating Legacy Systems with Microservices

As organizations transition to microservices architectures, they often face the challenge of integrating their existing legacy systems with the new, distributed service-oriented infrastructure. Legacy systems, which may consist of monolithic applications or older technologies, often serve as the backbone of many critical business processes. These systems, while reliable and well-established, were typically not designed to work in modern, distributed environments. Integrating legacy systems with microservices requires a thoughtful approach to ensure that the two can communicate effectively and that the transition is seamless, without disrupting business operations. The integration of legacy systems with microservices can unlock the benefits of modern architectures, such as scalability, flexibility, and faster development cycles, while still preserving the value of the existing investments in legacy technologies.

One of the primary challenges in integrating legacy systems with microservices is the difference in architectural styles. Legacy systems are typically monolithic, meaning that the entire application is built as a single unit where different modules or components are tightly coupled together. In contrast, microservices are designed to be loosely coupled, independently deployable units that communicate over well-defined APIs. This fundamental difference in architecture can make it difficult to directly connect legacy systems with microservices. However, by using appropriate integration patterns and strategies, organizations can bridge this gap and enable effective communication between the two systems.

One common approach to integrating legacy systems with microservices is the use of APIs. Legacy systems typically expose their functionality through legacy APIs, which are often monolithic and difficult to extend or adapt to modern use cases. To integrate these systems with microservices, organizations can build an API layer on top of the legacy system to enable communication with microservices. This API layer acts as a bridge, transforming the requests and responses between the legacy system and the microservices to ensure compatibility. This approach allows legacy systems to interact with modern microservices without requiring a complete rewrite of the legacy application. Over time, as the integration evolves, this API layer can be extended or replaced by more modern components, gradually decoupling the legacy system from the rest of the architecture.

Another approach to integrating legacy systems with microservices is the use of an event-driven architecture. In many cases, legacy systems rely on tightly coupled, synchronous communication, whereas microservices thrive in event-driven, asynchronous environments. By introducing an event-driven model, organizations can allow legacy systems to publish events, such as changes to business data or state, which microservices can then consume and react to. This decouples the systems and allows them to communicate asynchronously, making the integration more flexible and scalable. Event-driven architectures can be implemented using message brokers like Kafka, RabbitMQ, or AWS SNS, which facilitate communication between microservices and legacy systems by acting as intermediaries that handle event queues and message routing.

For legacy systems that have significant business logic and are critical to the organization, a common strategy is to wrap the legacy functionality in a microservice. This involves creating a new microservice that encapsulates the legacy functionality and exposes it via a modern API. Instead of directly modifying or replacing the legacy system, this approach preserves the existing system while making it accessible to the new microservices-based environment. Over time, this microservice can be refactored or replaced with a more modern implementation, but it allows the organization to continue using the legacy system while migrating to microservices gradually. This approach is particularly useful for organizations that need to maintain business continuity while transitioning to a more flexible and scalable architecture.

A more aggressive strategy for integrating legacy systems with microservices is to gradually replace legacy components with new microservices over time. This approach requires a detailed understanding of the business processes and the architecture of the legacy system, as well as careful planning to ensure that critical functionality is not disrupted during the migration. By identifying small, manageable chunks of the legacy system that can be replaced by microservices, organizations can incrementally move towards a fully microservices-based architecture. This "strangling" pattern involves creating new microservices alongside the legacy system, gradually moving the functionality of the legacy system into new services and then decommissioning the old code. This approach minimizes risk and allows the organization to continue operating as the transition occurs.

When integrating legacy systems with microservices, it is crucial to consider data management and consistency. Legacy systems often store data in monolithic databases that are tightly coupled with the application logic. In contrast, microservices typically have their own databases, ensuring loose coupling and autonomy. To integrate legacy systems with microservices, organizations must address how data will be shared between the two systems while maintaining data consistency. One approach is to use data replication or synchronization, where data from the legacy database is periodically replicated or synchronized with microservices databases. This ensures that both systems have access to the latest data without tightly coupling them. Another approach is to implement an event-driven architecture for data propagation, where changes in the legacy system are propagated as events to microservices, which then update their own databases accordingly. This approach allows each system to maintain its own data store while ensuring that the data remains consistent across both environments.

Security is another important consideration when integrating legacy systems with microservices. Legacy systems may use outdated or less secure authentication mechanisms, whereas modern microservices rely on more robust authentication protocols such as OAuth 2.0 or JSON Web Tokens (JWT). To integrate these systems securely, it is essential to implement an authentication and authorization layer that ensures that both the legacy system and the microservices adhere to modern security standards. This can involve using API gateways to enforce security policies, such as rate limiting, authentication, and encryption, ensuring that the communication between the legacy system and microservices remains secure.

Monitoring and observability are also essential aspects of integrating legacy systems with microservices. When dealing with a hybrid architecture, it is important to be able to track the health and performance of both the legacy system and the microservices. This requires implementing centralized logging, monitoring, and tracing systems that can collect data from both environments. Tools like Prometheus, Grafana, ELK Stack, and Jaeger can be used to collect and visualize metrics, logs, and traces from both the legacy systems and the microservices, providing a unified view of the overall system health. This is crucial for detecting issues, troubleshooting, and ensuring that the integration runs smoothly without disruptions.

Integrating legacy systems with microservices is not a one-size-fits-all approach, and organizations must carefully assess their specific needs and constraints before deciding on the best strategy. Whether by wrapping legacy systems with modern APIs, implementing event-driven architectures, or incrementally replacing legacy components with microservices, the goal is to create a seamless and flexible architecture that allows for innovation and scalability while preserving the value of existing systems. Through careful planning, gradual transitions, and the use of modern integration techniques, organizations can integrate legacy systems with microservices, unlocking the benefits of both worlds. This enables them to continue leveraging their legacy investments while embracing the advantages of microservices for the future.

Managing Microservices at Scale

As organizations adopt microservices architectures, they often begin by creating a handful of independent services that handle discrete pieces of functionality. Over time, however, these microservices grow in number and complexity, and managing them at scale becomes a significant challenge. At scale, microservices systems must be designed to handle large volumes of traffic, ensure high availability, and maintain performance across a growing number of services. Managing microservices at scale involves addressing a variety of operational concerns, such as service discovery, monitoring, resilience, security, and deployment. It requires careful planning, automation, and the right set of tools to ensure that the system remains stable, reliable, and easy to manage.

One of the first challenges when managing microservices at scale is service discovery. As the number of services grows, it becomes increasingly difficult to keep track of which services are running, where they are located, and how to route traffic to them. In a distributed microservices architecture, services are often deployed dynamically across a cluster of machines or containers. As services are added or removed, the system must be able to automatically discover and communicate with them. Service discovery tools like Consul, Eureka, or Kubernetes' built-in service discovery capabilities can help solve this problem by automatically registering services and updating the routing information as services are scaled up or down. With service discovery in place, microservices can find and communicate with one another without requiring manual intervention or hardcoded addresses, making the system more flexible and scalable.

As the number of microservices grows, monitoring and observability become critical to ensuring that the system remains healthy and performant. Microservices often span multiple servers or containers, making it challenging to track the performance of each individual service and the system as a whole. Effective monitoring involves collecting metrics such as request rates, response times, error rates, and resource utilization across all services, and visualizing this data to detect potential issues. Tools like Prometheus, Grafana, and Datadog are commonly used to collect and display these metrics, giving teams real-time visibility into the health of their microservices environment. In addition to metrics, centralized logging is essential for troubleshooting and debugging, as logs provide context about the events and errors occurring within services. Solutions like the ELK Stack (Elasticsearch, Logstash, Kibana) or Fluentd can aggregate logs from multiple services, making it easier to search, analyze, and correlate logs across the system.

Distributed tracing is another important aspect of managing microservices at scale. In a microservices architecture, requests often flow through multiple services, and understanding how they move through the system is essential for diagnosing issues and optimizing performance. Distributed tracing tools like Jaeger, Zipkin, and OpenTelemetry allow teams to trace the flow of requests as they pass through different services. These tools provide a visual representation of the request lifecycle, showing how long each service takes to process requests and where bottlenecks or delays occur. This level of insight helps teams identify performance issues, optimize service communication, and improve overall system efficiency.

At scale, resilience and fault tolerance are critical. Microservices systems are inherently distributed, and failures are inevitable. Whether due to network issues, service crashes, or resource exhaustion, microservices need to be designed to handle failures gracefully. One of the most important techniques for ensuring resilience in microservices is the implementation of retries, timeouts, and circuit breakers. Retries can automatically retry failed requests, ensuring that transient issues do not cause permanent failures. Timeouts can prevent requests from hanging indefinitely, ensuring that resources are not blocked. Circuit breakers, inspired by electrical circuit breakers, detect when a service is consistently failing and automatically stop further requests to that service, preventing cascading failures. Tools like Hystrix, Resilience4j, and Istio are commonly used to implement these patterns, ensuring that the system remains resilient even under adverse conditions.

Another important consideration when managing microservices at scale is security. As the number of services increases, so does the attack surface, making it more challenging to secure communication between services and protect sensitive data. In a microservices architecture, security must be implemented at multiple layers, including network security, service-to-service authentication, and access control. One of the most common approaches to securing microservices is to implement mutual TLS (Transport Layer Security) for encrypting communication between services and ensuring that both parties are authenticated. API gateways like Kong or Nginx can enforce security policies, such as rate limiting, authentication, and authorization, ensuring that only authorized services and users can access the system. Additionally, centralized identity and access management (IAM) systems, such as OAuth 2.0 or OpenID Connect, can be used to control access to services and protect sensitive data.

As the microservices architecture scales, managing deployments becomes increasingly complex. A microservices-based system typically involves frequent updates and deployments, as new features and bug fixes are delivered on a regular basis. Managing deployments at scale requires automation and coordination to ensure that services are updated consistently and reliably. Continuous integration (CI) and continuous delivery (CD) pipelines are essential for automating the build, testing, and deployment processes. Tools like Jenkins, GitLab CI, and CircleCI can be used to create CI/CD pipelines that automate the entire workflow from code commit to production deployment. Kubernetes, along with tools like Helm, can manage the deployment of microservices across a cluster, automating the scaling and rollout of new versions. Techniques like blue-green deployments and canary releases can be used to ensure that new versions of services are deployed with minimal disruption, allowing teams to test new features in production without affecting all users.

Scaling microservices is another key challenge that comes with managing systems at scale. Microservices should be designed to scale horizontally, meaning that additional instances of a service can be deployed to handle increased load. Tools like Kubernetes provide powerful features for automating the scaling of services based on demand, allowing microservices to scale in and out dynamically. Kubernetes uses horizontal pod autoscaling to automatically adjust the number of instances of a service based on resource usage metrics like CPU and memory. This ensures that microservices can handle fluctuating workloads and provide a responsive user experience. Additionally, containerization tools like Docker allow services to be packaged in a portable, standardized format, making it easier to deploy and scale services consistently across different environments.

Finally, managing microservices at scale requires a strong culture of collaboration between development, operations, and security teams. As the number of services grows, maintaining a high level of coordination and communication is essential to ensure that services are designed, deployed, and monitored effectively. DevOps practices, such as infrastructure as code, automation, and continuous monitoring, can help streamline operations and improve collaboration across teams. By adopting these practices and using the right set of tools, organizations can manage microservices at scale, ensuring that the system remains reliable, secure, and scalable as it grows.

Managing microservices at scale is a complex task that requires careful consideration of performance, resilience, security, and deployment. By using tools for service discovery, monitoring, resilience, security, and automation, organizations can ensure that their microservices systems remain stable and scalable, even as the number of services increases. Through automation and careful management, teams can maintain the health and performance of their microservices environments, allowing them to deliver reliable, high-quality services to their users.

Microservices in a Multi-Region Deployment

As organizations scale their microservices architectures to meet the demands of a global customer base, deploying microservices across multiple regions becomes an essential strategy. A multi-region deployment enables organizations to improve the availability, reliability, and performance of their services by leveraging geographically distributed data centers. By distributing microservices across different regions, organizations can ensure that their applications remain resilient, offer low-latency experiences to users, and are protected from regional failures that might otherwise disrupt service. However, managing microservices in a multi-region environment presents its own set of challenges, requiring careful consideration of architecture, data consistency, networking, and operational management. Understanding how to deploy and manage microservices in a multi-region context is crucial for organizations aiming to provide reliable and performant applications at scale.

One of the primary advantages of a multi-region deployment is improved fault tolerance. Microservices architectures are inherently distributed, and the failure of a single service or data center can affect the entire system. By deploying services across multiple regions, organizations can mitigate the impact of regional failures. If one region goes down due to network issues, natural disasters, or other disruptions, the system can automatically failover to another region that is still operational, ensuring that users experience minimal downtime. This is particularly important for businesses that rely on 24/7 availability and cannot afford to have their services interrupted. A well-designed multi-region deployment ensures that there is no single point of failure, increasing the overall reliability of the system and providing peace of mind to both the organization and its customers.

In addition to fault tolerance, multi-region deployments offer improved performance through reduced latency. By placing services closer to end-users, organizations can reduce the time it takes for requests to travel across the network. For example, a microservice deployed in a region that is geographically closer to a user's location will experience lower latency than a service located in a distant region. This can significantly improve the responsiveness of the application, providing a better user experience. For applications with a global user base, this performance boost is essential to keep pace with customer expectations for fast, real-time interactions. Multi-region deployment also allows organizations to optimize for regional traffic patterns, ensuring that services are better aligned with local demand.

Despite these benefits, managing microservices in a multi-region deployment introduces several complexities. One of the biggest challenges is ensuring data consistency across regions. In a microservices architecture, each service typically manages its own database, and the communication between services relies on asynchronous messaging or APIs. When services are deployed across multiple regions, it becomes necessary to synchronize data across those regions to ensure consistency. However, achieving strong consistency in a distributed environment is challenging due to network latency, partitioning, and the CAP theorem, which states that it is impossible to simultaneously achieve consistency, availability, and partition tolerance in distributed systems. As a result, organizations must make trade-offs between consistency and availability, choosing between eventual consistency, where data may take some time to synchronize across regions, and stronger consistency models that prioritize data accuracy at the cost of performance.

To handle data consistency in a multi-region deployment, many organizations adopt eventual consistency models, where updates to data in one region are propagated to other regions over time. Event-driven architectures and message queues such as Kafka or RabbitMQ can help facilitate this by enabling services to publish events whenever data changes, allowing other regions to subscribe to these events and update their local copies of the data. While eventual consistency ensures that the system can remain highly available and performant, it also introduces the possibility of temporary inconsistencies, which must be carefully managed. In some cases, organizations may use techniques like conflict resolution or versioning to address discrepancies that arise due to data being out-of-sync between regions.

Another key challenge in multi-region deployments is ensuring efficient service discovery and load balancing. In a single-region deployment, service discovery is relatively straightforward, as all services are within the same network. However, when microservices are deployed across multiple regions, it becomes necessary to manage the routing of requests to the appropriate service instances in the correct region. Load balancing must take into account factors such as the health of each region, the proximity of users, and regional failover requirements. Tools like Kubernetes, Istio, or cloud-native load balancers can be configured to support multi-region load balancing, automatically routing traffic to the region with the healthiest instances of a service and ensuring that requests are directed to the region that provides the best performance for the user.

In addition to load balancing, networking in a multi-region deployment must be carefully architected to ensure that services can communicate securely and efficiently across regions. This involves setting up virtual private networks (VPNs) or using cloud provider features like VPC peering or inter-region networking. Ensuring secure communication between regions requires the use of encryption protocols, such as TLS, to protect data in transit and to prevent unauthorized access. Multi-region architectures also require monitoring of network traffic to detect potential bottlenecks or issues with inter-region connectivity, ensuring that services can continue to interact with each other even as network conditions change.

Operationally, managing microservices in a multi-region environment requires additional tools and processes to monitor, alert, and automate tasks across regions. Tools like Prometheus, Grafana, and Datadog are essential for collecting and visualizing metrics from all regions, enabling teams to detect performance issues, failures, and resource bottlenecks. Centralized logging solutions, such as the ELK Stack or Fluentd, can aggregate logs from all regions, making it easier to troubleshoot issues and track the health of the system as a whole. Automated deployment tools like Helm, ArgoCD, or Terraform can be used to manage the deployment and scaling of services across multiple regions, ensuring that services are consistently and reliably deployed to the right regions based on demand.

Security is also a critical concern in multi-region deployments. With services spread across multiple data centers or cloud regions, ensuring that sensitive data is protected and that services are properly authenticated and authorized becomes more complex. Multi-region architectures require implementing strong security policies, such as role-based access control (RBAC), identity and access management (IAM), and encryption at rest and in transit. Additionally, organizations must be prepared to handle region-specific security compliance requirements, such as data residency laws or regional security standards. It is essential to regularly audit and monitor security policies to ensure that the system remains secure as the architecture scales and evolves.

Finally, disaster recovery and backup strategies must be adapted for multi-region deployments. While distributing services across regions improves fault tolerance, it also means that disaster recovery plans must account for failures in multiple locations. Organizations need to ensure that data is replicated across regions and that services can be quickly restored in the event of a regional failure. Backup and recovery strategies should be tested regularly, and automated failover mechanisms must be in place to minimize downtime and data loss in case of a regional disaster.

Managing microservices in a multi-region deployment is complex but highly beneficial for organizations seeking to provide high availability, scalability, and low-latency experiences to a global user base. By addressing challenges such as data consistency, service discovery, load balancing, networking, and security, organizations can ensure that their multi-region microservices architectures are resilient, performant, and secure. With the right tools and strategies, microservices can be deployed and managed effectively across regions, providing businesses with the flexibility and reliability needed to meet the demands of a global market.

Deploying Microservices in Edge Computing

Edge computing is an emerging paradigm that brings computation and data storage closer to the location where it is needed, typically near the source of data generation, such as IoT devices, sensors, or end-user devices. This approach addresses the limitations of cloud computing by reducing latency, improving bandwidth efficiency, and providing faster access to data for real-time processing. As microservices architectures continue to gain popularity for their flexibility and scalability, the integration of microservices with edge computing becomes an increasingly important strategy for organizations aiming to build highly responsive, decentralized, and efficient applications. Deploying microservices in edge computing environments presents unique challenges, but it also offers significant benefits in terms of performance, scalability, and reliability, especially in applications that require real-time data processing, high availability, and low-latency interactions.

In traditional cloud architectures, services are typically deployed in centralized data centers where resources are shared and scaled according to demand. However, as the number of devices and endpoints grows, particularly with the rise of IoT and mobile applications, cloud-based systems can face bottlenecks due to high latency and limited bandwidth. By processing data closer to where it is generated, edge computing allows for faster response times and reduces the need for extensive data transmission across the network. This is especially important for applications that require real-time processing, such as autonomous vehicles, industrial automation, and video streaming. In these cases, microservices deployed at the edge can handle local data processing, allowing for immediate insights and actions without having to send data back to a centralized cloud server.

One of the main advantages of deploying microservices in edge computing is the reduction in latency. Edge devices, such as gateways, routers, and local servers, are located geographically closer to the data sources, minimizing the time it takes for data to travel between the endpoint and the processing unit. By distributing microservices across edge locations, organizations can ensure that data processing happens as quickly as possible, which is crucial for time-sensitive applications. For example, in an industrial setting, edge computing can enable machines to process sensor data locally, allowing for immediate adjustments to machinery or systems based on real-time information, without waiting for data to travel to a central cloud server for analysis. This real-time processing capability enhances the overall performance and responsiveness of applications, providing users with a smoother experience.

Another key benefit of edge computing is the optimization of bandwidth usage. In cloud architectures, large volumes of data are often sent to centralized data centers for processing, which can lead to high network traffic and congestion, especially as the number of connected devices increases. By processing data locally at the edge, only relevant or summarized data needs to be transmitted to the cloud, reducing the amount of bandwidth required and minimizing network congestion. This is particularly useful for applications with limited bandwidth or remote locations where a high-speed internet connection is not available. By deploying microservices at the edge, organizations can ensure that they are using network resources more efficiently, while still being able to access cloud-based resources for storage, analytics, and long-term processing.

In addition to reducing latency and optimizing bandwidth, edge computing also offers greater reliability and fault tolerance. In cloud-based architectures, if a centralized data center experiences a failure, it can impact the entire system, resulting in service downtime and potential loss of data. Edge computing provides a more resilient approach by distributing services across multiple locations. If one edge device or gateway goes down, the system can continue to function using other nearby devices or services, ensuring that critical operations are not disrupted. For example, in a smart city application, multiple sensors may be collecting data from different locations. If one sensor or gateway fails, the remaining devices can continue to operate without affecting the overall system. This decentralization of processing and storage ensures that edge computing systems are more robust and capable of handling failures without causing widespread outages.

Deploying microservices at the edge also enables better data privacy and compliance with local regulations. With edge computing, data can be processed locally, which reduces the need for sensitive information to be transmitted over long distances or stored in centralized cloud servers. This can help organizations comply with data residency laws or privacy regulations, such as the General Data Protection Regulation (GDPR), which require data to be stored and processed within specific geographic regions. By deploying microservices at the edge, organizations can ensure that sensitive data remains within the local jurisdiction and is processed securely, while still benefiting from the flexibility and scalability of a microservices architecture.

However, deploying microservices in edge computing environments introduces several challenges that need to be carefully addressed. One of the primary challenges is managing the deployment and orchestration of microservices across a large number of geographically distributed edge devices. Unlike cloud-based environments, where centralized tools and services are used to manage the deployment and scaling of services, edge computing requires a more decentralized approach. Organizations must use specialized tools and platforms to manage the deployment, monitoring, and scaling of microservices at the edge. Technologies such as Kubernetes, Docker, and edge-specific orchestrators like K3s or OpenShift for edge environments can help manage the deployment of microservices across multiple edge nodes. These tools enable organizations to deploy, update, and monitor microservices across edge locations, ensuring that the system remains consistent and operational.

Another challenge of deploying microservices at the edge is ensuring security across distributed environments. Edge devices are often deployed in remote or less-secure locations, making them vulnerable to physical tampering or unauthorized access. Furthermore, securing communication between edge devices and the cloud or between different edge locations is critical for preventing data breaches or malicious attacks. To address these security concerns, organizations must implement robust encryption protocols, secure authentication mechanisms, and access controls. This includes ensuring that microservices deployed at the edge are isolated from one another and can only communicate through authorized channels. Additionally, using a secure API gateway at the edge can help manage access to microservices and enforce security policies.

Data consistency is another issue that must be managed when deploying microservices in edge environments. Since microservices at the edge may process data locally and asynchronously, ensuring that data remains consistent across the entire system can be challenging. In edge computing, data can be generated and processed locally, but it must be synchronized with the central cloud or other edge devices to maintain consistency across the entire system. Event-driven architectures, message queues, and synchronization protocols can be used to ensure that updates are propagated across edge devices and the cloud, allowing for consistent and accurate data.

Lastly, managing the lifecycle of microservices at the edge requires careful planning and monitoring. Edge devices often have limited computing resources compared to cloud servers, which means that microservices deployed at the edge must be lightweight and optimized for performance. In addition, edge devices may have intermittent connectivity to the cloud, requiring microservices to be resilient to connectivity issues and capable of functioning in a disconnected mode. Ensuring that microservices can operate efficiently in these conditions requires advanced monitoring, logging, and automated management tools to ensure that the system remains operational even when devices or services are offline.

Deploying microservices in edge computing environments offers significant benefits, including reduced latency, optimized bandwidth usage, improved reliability, and enhanced data privacy. By leveraging edge computing, organizations can build responsive, decentralized applications that provide real-time processing capabilities and scale efficiently across global regions. However, successfully managing microservices at the edge requires addressing challenges related to deployment, security, data consistency, and resource management. With the right tools and strategies, organizations can harness the power of edge computing to deliver high-performance, reliable, and secure applications that meet the demands of modern, distributed systems.

Data Consistency and Integrity in Microservices

As organizations adopt microservices architectures, one of the most significant challenges they face is maintaining data consistency and integrity across distributed services. Microservices break down applications into smaller, independently deployable services that each manage their own data stores. While this decentralization promotes flexibility, scalability, and resilience, it also complicates the management of data consistency and integrity. In traditional monolithic applications, consistency is often simpler to achieve because the entire application operates within a single database, ensuring that data is always up-to-date and consistent across the system. However, in a microservices architecture, each service may have its own database, and services need to interact with one another over the network, making it more difficult to maintain consistency across the system. This is particularly important in systems where data integrity is critical, such as in financial applications, healthcare systems, or e-commerce platforms.

The first challenge of data consistency in microservices is ensuring that the data stored in different services remains synchronized. Since each microservice typically manages its own database, there is a need for effective communication between services to ensure that data is consistent and up-to-date across the entire system. Microservices architectures typically rely on asynchronous communication patterns, such as event-driven messaging, to propagate changes between services. When one service updates its data, it can emit an event that other services listen for, allowing them to update their own state accordingly. This approach allows for decoupling between services, but it introduces the challenge of eventual consistency. Eventual consistency means that the system may not be consistent at all times, but over time, the data will converge to a consistent state. This can be acceptable in many cases, but it is essential to carefully manage and monitor the process to avoid situations where the system's data is inconsistent for too long, potentially causing errors or unexpected behavior.

One approach to managing consistency across microservices is to use the Saga pattern. The Saga pattern is a way of managing long-running business transactions that span multiple services. Instead of using traditional distributed transactions that require strong consistency across all services, the Saga pattern breaks a transaction into a series of smaller, compensatable steps. Each step is handled by a different service, and if any step fails, the pattern ensures that the preceding steps are rolled back, preserving the integrity of the system. This approach allows for flexibility in managing complex workflows, while still ensuring that data remains consistent even in the face of failures. By using the Saga pattern, organizations can avoid the need for distributed locking or other heavyweight mechanisms that could reduce system performance and scalability.

Another approach to maintaining data consistency in microservices is to adopt the principle of "bounded contexts." A bounded context refers to the explicit boundaries within which a service operates and manages its own data. Each microservice is responsible for maintaining the integrity of its own data and ensuring that it is consistent within its boundaries. When services need to communicate with each other, they do so via well-defined APIs or event streams, which are designed to ensure that data is correctly synchronized. Bounded contexts help to minimize dependencies between services, reducing the chances of conflicts or inconsistencies arising from shared data. In practice, this means that a service may be allowed to operate independently and be more resilient to failures or changes in other parts of the system. However, this approach also requires careful design to ensure that services communicate effectively and maintain the overall coherence of the system.

Despite the benefits of eventual consistency and bounded contexts, there are still cases where strong consistency is required. For example, in financial systems, it is often necessary to ensure that transactions are processed in a strictly consistent order to avoid issues such as double spending or data corruption. In such cases, distributed transaction protocols like two-phase commit (2PC) or atomic operations may be used to ensure that all participants in a transaction are in agreement before the changes are committed. However, these protocols can introduce complexity and performance overhead, as they require coordination between multiple services to ensure that the transaction is committed consistently. For this reason, it is important to carefully evaluate the need for strong consistency in each service and determine the appropriate level of consistency required for the application.

Data integrity is another critical concern in microservices architectures. Ensuring data integrity means that the data in each service remains accurate, valid, and consistent over time. This involves validating input data to ensure it conforms to expected formats and business rules, as well as ensuring that the data is correctly persisted in the database. In a distributed system, maintaining data integrity can be more challenging due to the decentralized nature of services and the potential for network failures or data corruption. One way to enforce data integrity is by using techniques such as validation patterns and consistency checks. For example, when a service receives data from an external source, it can perform input validation to ensure that the data is correct and meets the necessary constraints. This helps to catch errors early and prevents invalid data from being propagated through the system.

Another technique for ensuring data integrity is implementing idempotency, particularly in systems that rely on retries or asynchronous communication. Idempotency ensures that repeated operations, such as the processing of the same request multiple times, do not result in inconsistent or duplicated data. This is particularly important in microservices architectures, where network failures or timeouts can lead to requests being retried. By using idempotent operations, services can ensure that even if a request is processed multiple times, the resulting data remains consistent and correct. Techniques such as unique request identifiers or versioning of requests can be used to implement idempotency, ensuring that the same request is not processed more than once.

In addition to these strategies, organizations must consider the implications of distributed data stores when managing data consistency and integrity. In a microservices architecture, each service may have its own database, which could be a relational database, NoSQL database, or even a distributed database. Ensuring consistency and integrity across these different data stores can be difficult, especially when services are operating in different geographic locations or when the data is being replicated. Techniques such as event sourcing, where changes to data are stored as events that can be replayed to reconstruct the current state, can help maintain data integrity in distributed environments. Event sourcing allows for a clear audit trail of all changes, ensuring that any inconsistencies can be traced back to their source and corrected.

Ultimately, managing data consistency and integrity in microservices is a complex challenge that requires careful consideration of the specific needs of each service and the overall system. By adopting patterns like the Saga pattern, bounded contexts, and idempotent operations, organizations can ensure that data remains consistent and accurate across services. Additionally, techniques like input validation, event sourcing, and distributed transactions can help enforce data integrity, even in the face of network failures or distributed data stores. While eventual consistency may be sufficient for many use cases, it is important to carefully evaluate the need for strong consistency in each service and design the system accordingly. By addressing these concerns proactively, organizations can build microservices architectures that maintain high levels of data consistency and integrity, while also providing the flexibility and scalability that microservices are known for.

Transaction Management in Distributed Microservices

In a microservices architecture, transaction management presents unique challenges due to the decentralized nature of the system. Unlike monolithic applications, where a single transaction typically spans one database, microservices often involve multiple services, each with its own database. These services operate independently, and transactions often need to span across different services, making it more complex to manage consistency, reliability, and fault tolerance. Effective transaction management in distributed microservices requires addressing these challenges and ensuring that the system remains robust, resilient, and performant while maintaining the integrity of data across all services.

In a traditional monolithic system, transactions are typically handled using a single, centralized database. This makes it relatively easy to ensure that all operations within the transaction are either fully completed or fully rolled back in the case of failure. However, in a microservices architecture, where each service manages its own database and operates independently, traditional database transactions such as ACID (Atomicity, Consistency, Isolation, Durability) transactions cannot be used in the same way. This is because services need to communicate over a network, and network failures or delays can lead to inconsistent states if a transaction spans multiple services. In addition, the concept of a single transactional boundary is no longer applicable, as services are distributed and can be independently scaled and managed.

One of the key principles of transaction management in distributed microservices is ensuring consistency across all services involved in a transaction. In the context of microservices, there are different approaches to achieving consistency, each with its own trade-offs. The two most commonly used approaches are eventual consistency and strong consistency. Eventual consistency allows for the system to reach a consistent state over time, even if the services involved in a transaction are temporarily out of sync. This approach is often suitable for many use cases, where the system can tolerate some delay in consistency. On the other hand, strong consistency requires that all services involved in a transaction be in sync at all times, which can be difficult to achieve in a distributed system but may be necessary for applications with strict data integrity requirements, such as financial systems.

One of the most widely adopted patterns for managing transactions in distributed microservices is the Saga pattern. The Saga pattern breaks down a distributed transaction into a series of smaller, manageable steps that are coordinated across different services. Each step of the saga is a local transaction within a single service, and the overall transaction is considered complete when all steps have been successfully completed. If any step fails, compensating actions are taken to undo the changes made by the previous steps. This ensures that the system remains in a consistent state, even in the case of failures. The Saga pattern is particularly useful for long-running transactions that span multiple services, such as order processing or booking systems. It allows for greater flexibility and resilience in the system, as it avoids the need for distributed locks or complex coordination mechanisms between services.

There are two main types of sagas: choreography-based and orchestration-based. In a choreography-based saga, each service involved in the transaction knows what to do next and communicates directly with other services to move the transaction forward. This approach is highly decentralized and requires minimal central coordination, as each service is responsible for executing its part of the transaction and notifying others when it has completed its task. However, this approach can become complex as the number of services grows, as each service must handle the logic for the next step in the transaction.

In an orchestration-based saga, a central coordinator or orchestrator service is responsible for controlling the flow of the transaction. The orchestrator sends commands to the services involved in the transaction, ensuring that each step is completed in the correct order. This approach offers more centralized control, making it easier to manage and monitor the transaction. However, it can create a single point of failure if the orchestrator service becomes unavailable, and it may require additional infrastructure to manage the coordination of services.

While the Saga pattern is a powerful solution for handling long-running transactions in microservices, there are other strategies for ensuring data consistency and integrity. One such strategy is the use of event-driven architectures, where services communicate via events rather than direct API calls. When a service performs an action, such as updating its data, it emits an event that other services can listen for and react to. This enables asynchronous communication between services and allows them to maintain consistency without being tightly coupled. Event-driven architectures are well-suited to microservices, as they allow for better scalability and decoupling of services. However, they also introduce challenges around ensuring that events are processed in the correct order and handling the potential for events to be missed or processed out of order.

Another important aspect of transaction management in distributed microservices is handling failures. In a distributed system, failures are inevitable, whether due to network issues, service crashes, or resource exhaustion. To ensure that transactions can be completed reliably, microservices must be designed to handle failures gracefully. This can be done by implementing retries, timeouts, and circuit breakers to protect the system from cascading failures. Retries automatically attempt to process a failed transaction again, while timeouts ensure that services do not wait indefinitely for a response. Circuit breakers detect when a service is failing and stop further requests to that service, allowing it to recover without affecting the rest of the system.

Idempotency is another key consideration in transaction management for microservices. Idempotency ensures that repeated requests do not result in inconsistent or duplicate data. For example, if a service receives the same request multiple times, it should return the same result without causing any unintended side effects. This is especially important in distributed systems where network failures can lead to requests being retried, potentially causing the same operation to be performed multiple times. By designing idempotent operations, services can ensure that data consistency is maintained even in the face of retries or message duplication.

In addition to handling failures, it is essential to consider the isolation of transactions in a distributed environment. In traditional database systems, transactions are isolated, meaning that the changes made by one transaction are not visible to other transactions until the transaction is complete. In a distributed system, achieving this level of isolation can be difficult due to the challenges of coordinating changes across multiple services. One approach to managing transaction isolation is to use compensation logic, where changes made by a service are rolled back if the transaction fails at any point. This helps ensure that the system maintains a consistent state, even if a transaction is only partially completed.

Finally, transaction management in distributed microservices requires a strong monitoring and observability framework to detect and resolve issues quickly. Tools such as distributed tracing, centralized logging, and real-time metrics allow teams to track the flow of transactions across services and identify bottlenecks or failures. By integrating monitoring and observability tools into the transaction management process, organizations can ensure that transactions are processed correctly and that issues are quickly detected and resolved before they affect the system's performance or data integrity.

Managing transactions in a distributed microservices architecture is inherently complex due to the decentralized nature of the system and the need for services to coordinate over a network. The use of patterns such as the Saga pattern, event-driven architectures, and techniques like idempotency and compensation logic can help organizations handle long-running transactions and maintain data consistency and integrity across services. Additionally, failure handling mechanisms, such as retries, timeouts, and circuit breakers, are essential to ensure that transactions can be completed reliably even in the face of network or service failures. By combining these strategies with strong monitoring and observability, organizations can manage transactions in distributed microservices systems effectively, ensuring data consistency and integrity while providing high levels of availability and performance.

Microservices and Security Authentication Methods

In the world of modern application architectures, microservices have gained widespread popularity due to their flexibility, scalability, and ease of development. A microservices architecture involves breaking down a large, monolithic application into smaller, independently deployable services that communicate with each other over well-defined APIs. While this approach offers numerous benefits, it also introduces unique security challenges, particularly when it comes to authentication. Microservices often need to handle complex interactions between services and users, each of which may have different authentication and authorization requirements. Managing these interactions securely across multiple services can be daunting, requiring effective authentication mechanisms to ensure that only authorized entities can access the system. Understanding the various authentication methods available and how they can be integrated into a microservices architecture is crucial for building secure systems.

One of the most commonly used authentication methods in microservices is token-based authentication, specifically using JSON Web Tokens (JWT). In a typical microservices setup, each service is responsible for handling its own authentication, and the authentication mechanism needs to be decentralized to allow services to communicate independently. JWT is a popular choice because it allows for stateless authentication. Instead of relying on a centralized session store or database, the authentication information is embedded within the token itself. This token is issued when a user logs in and contains information such as the user's identity and permissions, which can be verified by any service that receives the token. Since JWT is self-contained and signed by the issuer, it ensures that the data within the token cannot be tampered with. This allows microservices to authenticate requests without needing to query a central authentication service every time a request is made, reducing the overhead and latency associated with authentication.

The process typically involves an initial login where the user provides their credentials (such as a username and password). If the credentials are valid, the authentication service issues a JWT token, which the user can then use to authenticate subsequent requests to other microservices. Each microservice can validate the token by checking its signature and decoding its payload, which contains the necessary claims and information. This decentralization of authentication allows microservices to operate independently while still ensuring that the user's identity is securely verified.

Another widely used authentication method in microservices is OAuth 2.0. OAuth 2.0 is a delegation protocol that allows third-party applications to access resources without exposing user credentials. In the context of microservices, OAuth 2.0 is often used to authenticate users by delegating authentication to an external identity provider, such as Google, Facebook, or an enterprise identity provider. OAuth 2.0 is commonly used in scenarios where users need to authenticate with external services or APIs. The process typically involves obtaining an access token from the identity provider, which is then used to authenticate subsequent requests to microservices. This approach is particularly useful in systems where users need to be authenticated across multiple platforms or services, as it allows for a single sign-on (SSO) experience.

OAuth 2.0 is built around the concept of access tokens, which are granted to clients after they authenticate with the identity provider. These tokens can be used to access resources on behalf of the user, and they usually have an expiration time, which enhances security by ensuring that tokens are not valid indefinitely. OAuth 2.0 also supports scopes, which define the specific permissions associated with the access token. For example, a token issued for accessing a user's profile data may have a different scope than a token issued for accessing their financial data. By defining and enforcing scopes, OAuth 2.0 provides fine-grained control over what each service can do on behalf of the user.

While JWT and OAuth 2.0 are commonly used in microservices architectures, there are also other authentication mechanisms that can be utilized, depending on the specific security requirements. One such method is Mutual TLS (mTLS), a security protocol that provides two-way authentication between clients and servers. In mTLS, both the client and the server are required to authenticate each other using digital certificates. This is particularly useful in service-to-service communication within a microservices environment, where services need to communicate securely with one another. mTLS ensures that both parties are authenticated before establishing a secure connection, preventing unauthorized access to sensitive data. mTLS is often used in conjunction with other authentication methods like JWT to ensure that both the user and the services are properly authenticated.

In a typical microservices architecture, communication between services can be over HTTP or gRPC, and securing this communication is critical to prevent unauthorized access or data breaches. In addition to mTLS, mutual authentication can be achieved using API keys, which are another common authentication method. API keys are typically used to authenticate services and allow them to make API requests to other services. Each service is issued a unique API key, which it includes in the request headers when making API calls. The receiving service can then validate the API key to ensure that the request is coming from an authorized source. While API keys are easy to implement, they are generally less secure than other methods, such as JWT or mTLS, as they can be easily intercepted if not properly encrypted.

In addition to authentication, authorization plays a critical role in securing microservices. Authentication ensures that a user or service is who they claim to be, but authorization ensures that they are allowed to perform the requested action. One common approach to authorization in microservices is Role-Based Access Control (RBAC), which defines permissions based on user roles. For example, a user with an "admin" role may have access to all microservices, while a user with a "user" role may have restricted access to certain services. RBAC can be implemented by attaching roles to the JWT token or by using an external authorization service that validates the user's permissions based on their role before granting access to a resource.

Another approach to authorization is Attribute-Based Access Control (ABAC), which provides more fine-grained control over access based on attributes such as the user's location, the time of day, or the type of request being made. ABAC allows for dynamic policies to be enforced, where access is granted or denied based on a variety of contextual factors, rather than predefined roles. This makes ABAC more flexible and adaptable to complex access control scenarios in microservices environments.

As microservices architectures scale, the need for centralized authentication and authorization management becomes even more critical. Managing authentication and authorization at the service level for each microservice can become cumbersome and error-prone. To address this, many organizations adopt an API Gateway or an Identity and Access Management (IAM) solution that acts as a central point for authentication and authorization. The API Gateway handles all incoming requests, authenticates users, and enforces authorization policies before forwarding the requests to the appropriate microservices. This reduces the complexity of managing authentication across multiple services and provides a single point of control for security policies.

Securing authentication in microservices environments requires a combination of methods to ensure that both users and services are properly authenticated and authorized. Token-based authentication, OAuth 2.0, mutual TLS, and API keys are all widely used techniques, each with its strengths and weaknesses. As microservices architectures grow, it becomes essential to manage authentication and authorization centrally and ensure that security policies are consistently enforced across all services. With the right combination of authentication mechanisms and best practices in place, organizations can build secure and scalable microservices systems that protect sensitive data while providing users with the flexibility and functionality they need.

Role of APIs in Microservices Integration

In the realm of modern software development, microservices have emerged as a powerful architectural approach, breaking down large, monolithic applications into smaller, independent services. These services are designed to perform a specific business function and communicate with each other to form a cohesive system. The key enabler of this communication and integration between microservices is the use of Application Programming Interfaces (APIs). APIs provide the means for different services to interact, exchange data, and perform operations in a standardized way, ensuring that the microservices can work together while maintaining their independence. Understanding the role of APIs in microservices integration is critical for designing scalable, reliable, and efficient systems that can meet the demands of modern applications.

At its core, an API defines a set of rules and protocols that govern how services interact with each other. In microservices architectures, APIs are the contract that allows different services, often developed and deployed independently, to communicate over well-defined interfaces. These interfaces abstract the underlying complexities of the services, enabling them to interact seamlessly without being tightly coupled. For example, one service might expose an API that allows another service to retrieve information, perform an operation, or trigger a specific action. The microservices themselves do not need to know the internal workings of each other; they only need to know how to communicate through the API.

APIs are essential in microservices integration because they provide the necessary abstraction layer that decouples services from one another. This decoupling allows for greater flexibility and scalability. Microservices can evolve independently as long as the API contract remains consistent. For instance, a service's internal logic may change, or its implementation may be replaced with a completely different technology stack, but as long as the API interface remains the same, other services that interact with it will not be affected. This ability to update and scale services independently is one of the key advantages of microservices architectures.

One of the most important aspects of APIs in microservices integration is that they enable loose coupling between services. This loose coupling is crucial for ensuring that changes in one service do not have unintended ripple effects on other services. By providing a well-defined API for interaction, each microservice can be developed, deployed, and maintained independently. This independence allows teams to work on different services simultaneously, improving development efficiency and reducing the complexity of managing a large, monolithic codebase. Additionally, this decoupling makes it easier to scale individual services based on demand without affecting the entire system.

APIs in microservices can take different forms depending on the nature of the interaction and the protocols used. The most common types of APIs in microservices integration are RESTful APIs and gRPC (Google Remote Procedure Call). RESTful APIs are based on HTTP and are widely used in microservices because of their simplicity, flexibility, and compatibility with web technologies. REST APIs allow services to communicate using standard HTTP methods like GET, POST, PUT, and DELETE, which are mapped to the appropriate operations in the service. REST APIs also typically use JSON or XML as data formats for exchanging information, making them easy to understand and integrate with other systems.

On the other hand, gRPC is a more performance-oriented protocol developed by Google, designed for high-throughput, low-latency communication between services. It uses Protocol Buffers (protobufs) for data serialization, which is more compact and efficient than JSON or XML, making it ideal for environments where speed and efficiency are critical. gRPC is often used in microservices that require real-time communication or need to handle high volumes of data, such as in IoT systems or microservices that perform intensive computations.

In addition to these communication protocols, APIs in microservices architectures often include mechanisms for handling authentication and authorization. Security is a critical concern in any distributed system, and microservices architectures are no exception. Since microservices often interact over the internet or internal networks, APIs must be secured to prevent unauthorized access and ensure that data remains protected. Common approaches to securing APIs in microservices include using OAuth 2.0 for authorization and JSON Web Tokens (JWT) for secure token-based authentication. These mechanisms ensure that only authorized services and users can access sensitive data or perform specific actions within the system.

APIs also play a vital role in facilitating service discovery, a key aspect of managing microservices at scale. In a large microservices environment, services are constantly being added, removed, or scaled up and down, which can make it difficult for other services to locate and communicate with the right instances. To address this, microservices architectures often rely on service discovery tools, which allow services to register themselves and discover other services dynamically. APIs act as the interface through which services can register with a service registry, such as Consul or Eureka, and query it to find available instances of other services. This automatic discovery ensures that microservices can continue to function even as the underlying infrastructure changes.

Another critical role that APIs play in microservices integration is enabling communication between microservices across different environments and platforms. Microservices often span multiple data centers or even public and private cloud environments, and they may be built using different programming languages or frameworks. APIs provide a standardized way to connect these heterogeneous services, allowing them to communicate and share data regardless of the underlying technologies. For example, a microservice running in a Kubernetes cluster may need to communicate with a service running in a public cloud, such as AWS or Azure. APIs abstract away the complexities of these different environments, allowing services to interact seamlessly.

Moreover, the management of APIs in microservices architectures is essential for ensuring that the integration between services remains smooth and efficient. API gateways are commonly used to manage and route requests between services. An API gateway acts as a single entry point for all incoming traffic, directing requests to the appropriate microservice based on the request's parameters. It also handles tasks such as load balancing, request routing, security enforcement, rate limiting, and caching. By using an API gateway, organizations can centralize common tasks, such as authentication and logging, and ensure that API calls are properly managed and monitored. This approach also simplifies the process of scaling microservices by providing a unified interface through which services can communicate, without needing to manage individual service endpoints directly.

One of the most significant benefits of APIs in microservices integration is that they allow for the evolution of the system without disrupting the overall architecture. As microservices need to evolve independently, the API contracts can remain consistent while the underlying services are updated or replaced. This ability to change and upgrade services without affecting the entire system is a key advantage of microservices over monolithic architectures, where changes to one part of the application can often have far-reaching consequences.

APIs are a cornerstone of microservices integration, enabling communication, flexibility, and scalability within a distributed system. By providing a standardized interface for services to interact, APIs allow microservices to remain decoupled, which improves the maintainability and scalability of the system. The use of secure, well-defined APIs ensures that services can communicate efficiently and reliably, even in large-scale and complex environments. With the right tools and best practices in place, APIs enable microservices architectures to evolve and grow, allowing organizations to build more resilient, agile, and efficient systems that meet the needs of modern software development.

Managing Microservices with Kubernetes Operators

Kubernetes has become the de facto standard for container orchestration, allowing organizations to automate the deployment, scaling, and management of containerized applications. As microservices architectures continue to grow in complexity, managing these applications effectively at scale becomes increasingly difficult. Kubernetes provides a robust framework for managing microservices, and one of the most powerful tools within Kubernetes is the concept of Operators. Operators are a way of extending Kubernetes to manage the lifecycle of complex applications, including microservices, in a more automated and scalable manner. They provide a method for handling tasks such as deployment, scaling, upgrades, and failure recovery, ensuring that microservices run efficiently and reliably.

Operators are essentially Kubernetes controllers that use custom resources to manage the lifecycle of an application. They are designed to automate tasks that would otherwise require manual intervention or custom scripts. By defining an Operator for a particular microservice or application, organizations can encapsulate the logic needed to manage that service within Kubernetes, allowing Kubernetes to handle the complex operational tasks automatically. This approach helps simplify the management of microservices and reduces the operational burden on teams, allowing them to focus more on development and innovation rather than manual configuration and maintenance.

The key benefit of using Kubernetes Operators for microservices management is the ability to automate the deployment and management of services in a way that is both repeatable and scalable. Traditional approaches to managing microservices often involve writing custom scripts or using external tools to handle tasks such as scaling, deployment, and failure recovery. These approaches can become cumbersome and difficult to maintain as the number of services increases. Operators, on the other hand, allow organizations to define their desired state for each microservice and let Kubernetes handle the rest. For example, an Operator can be configured to automatically deploy a microservice whenever a new version is released, ensuring that the system is always running the latest version without requiring manual intervention.

In addition to automating deployment, Kubernetes Operators are also valuable for managing the scaling of microservices. In a microservices architecture, services often need to scale up or down based on demand. Kubernetes provides native support for scaling, but Operators can extend this functionality by defining custom scaling logic that is specific to the application's requirements. For instance, an Operator can be configured to scale a service based on metrics such as CPU usage, request rate, or custom application-specific metrics. This allows microservices to automatically scale according to their specific needs, ensuring that the system remains responsive under varying loads.

Failure recovery is another area where Kubernetes Operators can significantly improve the management of microservices. In a large-scale microservices environment, failures are inevitable, and it is crucial to have mechanisms in place to recover from these failures automatically. Kubernetes provides basic mechanisms for handling failures, such as pod restarts, but Operators allow for more sophisticated recovery strategies. For example, an Operator can monitor the health of a microservice and, in the event of a failure, initiate a rollback to a previous stable version or automatically redeploy the service with updated configurations. Operators can also handle more complex failure scenarios, such as coordinating the recovery of multiple interdependent microservices, ensuring that the system remains consistent and operational.

Kubernetes Operators also play a crucial role in managing the lifecycle of microservices, particularly when it comes to upgrades and patching. In a microservices architecture, services are constantly evolving, with new versions being released to introduce features, fix bugs, or address security vulnerabilities. Managing upgrades manually can be time-consuming and error-prone, especially when dealing with complex interdependencies between services. Operators can automate the upgrade process, ensuring that microservices are updated in a controlled and predictable manner. For instance, an Operator can handle the rollout of a new version of a microservice, ensuring that the update is applied to the appropriate number of instances while maintaining system availability. Operators can also be used to manage rolling updates, allowing microservices to be upgraded gradually to minimize the risk of downtime or service disruption.

Another significant advantage of using Kubernetes Operators is their ability to manage the configuration and secrets associated with microservices. In a microservices environment, services often require sensitive information such as API keys, database credentials, and other configuration settings to function correctly. Managing these secrets securely is a critical concern, as exposing sensitive information can lead to security vulnerabilities. Kubernetes provides native support for managing secrets through Kubernetes Secrets, but Operators can extend this functionality by automating the management of configuration and secrets across multiple microservices. For example, an Operator can be used to automatically inject the necessary configuration values into the microservices at runtime, ensuring that they are always using the correct settings without requiring manual intervention.

Operators can also help manage the complex dependencies between microservices. In many cases, microservices are dependent on other services to function correctly. For instance, a service may require access to a database, a cache, or a messaging system in order to perform its tasks. Managing these dependencies manually can be cumbersome, especially as the number of microservices grows. Operators can automate the process of configuring and managing these dependencies, ensuring that each service has access to the necessary resources when it is deployed. This reduces the complexity of managing interdependencies and helps ensure that the system remains consistent and functional even as services are updated or replaced.

One of the challenges of using Kubernetes Operators for microservices management is the need to develop custom logic for each service. While Kubernetes provides a powerful set of features for managing containers, Operators require developers to write custom code that defines how each service should be deployed, scaled, and managed. This can require significant effort, particularly when dealing with complex services or applications. However, the benefits of automation, scalability, and reliability that Operators provide often outweigh the initial development cost. Furthermore, there are many open-source Operators available that can be used as templates or starting points for building custom Operators, reducing the amount of code that needs to be written from scratch.

Kubernetes Operators are a powerful tool for managing microservices at scale, providing a way to automate the deployment, scaling, failure recovery, and lifecycle management of services. By leveraging Operators, organizations can reduce the operational burden of managing microservices, ensuring that they remain reliable, efficient, and scalable as they grow. Operators enable microservices to evolve and scale independently, making it easier to manage complex, distributed systems. As the adoption of Kubernetes and microservices continues to rise, Operators will play an increasingly critical role in simplifying the management of modern, containerized applications, allowing organizations to focus on delivering value to their users while maintaining a high level of system reliability and performance.

Handling Cross-Cutting Concerns in Microservices

In a microservices architecture, an application is broken down into small, independently deployable services, each responsible for a specific business capability. While this approach provides numerous advantages such as scalability, flexibility, and easier maintenance, it also introduces significant challenges, especially when it comes to managing cross-cutting concerns. Cross-cutting concerns are aspects of an application that affect multiple services but do not belong to any single service's core business logic. These concerns include logging, authentication, authorization, security, monitoring, data consistency, error handling, and configuration management. Managing these concerns effectively is crucial for maintaining the system's overall reliability, security, and performance. Given that microservices often operate independently, it becomes essential to handle cross-cutting concerns in a way that ensures consistency across all services without introducing unnecessary complexity.

One of the most common approaches to handling cross-cutting concerns in microservices is by using centralized mechanisms that abstract away the implementation details from individual services. This approach reduces the need for each service to independently implement the same functionality, simplifying development and reducing the risk of inconsistencies across services. For instance, logging is a typical cross-cutting concern. Each microservice needs to log information related to its execution, errors, and interactions with other services. Without centralized logging, it would be difficult to correlate logs across multiple services, making troubleshooting and monitoring challenging. Centralized logging solutions like the ELK stack (Elasticsearch, Logstash, Kibana), Fluentd, or Splunk aggregate logs from all microservices into a single system where they can be easily queried and analyzed. This enables a holistic view of the application, helping teams quickly identify performance bottlenecks, errors, and security issues.

Authentication and authorization are another critical cross-cutting concern in microservices environments. As each microservice handles a specific piece of functionality, users must authenticate to interact with any service, and access controls must be enforced across the system. Managing authentication and authorization at the service level can quickly become complex and error-prone. Instead, a more centralized approach can be employed by using an API Gateway or Identity and Access Management (IAM) solutions. The API Gateway acts as a gatekeeper for all incoming requests, authenticating users and ensuring that only authorized users can access specific services. OAuth 2.0 and JSON Web Tokens (JWT) are commonly used for implementing secure, token-based authentication and authorization in a centralized manner. By implementing these solutions at the API Gateway level, microservices can focus on their core business logic without worrying about handling user authentication and permissions individually. This also simplifies scaling, as the authentication and authorization logic remains consistent across all services.

Security, as a cross-cutting concern, is paramount in any system, but it is especially critical in a microservices architecture. Since microservices often interact over a network, securing communication between services is vital to protect against malicious attacks and data breaches. Encryption, both at rest and in transit, is essential for maintaining confidentiality. Secure communication protocols such as HTTPS, coupled with mutual TLS (mTLS), can be employed to secure communication between services. mTLS provides two-way authentication, ensuring that both the client and server are authenticated before any data is exchanged. This is particularly useful in service-to-service communication, where microservices need to ensure that the services they are communicating with are trusted. Additionally, security can be enhanced further by using centralized security services or frameworks like Istio, which provides comprehensive security features, including access control, encryption, and observability, to ensure that the system remains secure across multiple services.

Monitoring is another cross-cutting concern that becomes even more critical in a microservices environment due to the distributed nature of the architecture. Monitoring ensures that the system is functioning as expected, and it provides the necessary data for troubleshooting and optimizing performance. Since microservices run independently, each microservice needs to be monitored individually, but it is also important to have a centralized monitoring solution that gives a unified view of the entire system. Tools like Prometheus and Grafana are commonly used for collecting and visualizing metrics such as request rates, error rates, response times, and system resource utilization. Distributed tracing tools like Jaeger or Zipkin can track requests as they flow through multiple microservices, providing detailed insights into how different services interact and where performance bottlenecks occur. Centralized monitoring allows teams to proactively address issues, ensuring that services remain performant and reliable across the system.

Data consistency across services is another significant cross-cutting concern in microservices. Since each service in a microservices architecture manages its own database, ensuring that data is consistent across all services can be challenging. In traditional monolithic applications, a single database can be used, ensuring consistency through ACID transactions. However, in microservices, where each service is responsible for its own data store, distributed transactions become more complex. Eventual consistency is often the solution in microservices architectures, where changes in one service are propagated to other services through events or messages. Event-driven architectures, utilizing message brokers like Kafka or RabbitMQ, are commonly used to ensure that services can stay synchronized. By emitting events when data changes, services can subscribe to these events and update their own data stores, ensuring that all services eventually reach a consistent state, even though they may temporarily be out of sync.

Error handling and resilience are also critical cross-cutting concerns that must be managed in microservices architectures. Since microservices are distributed and independently deployable, individual services can fail for various reasons, such as network issues, resource exhaustion, or application bugs. To ensure that the overall system remains operational in the face of failures, microservices need to implement fault tolerance mechanisms. One common approach is the use of circuit breakers, which prevent cascading failures by detecting when a service is failing and temporarily halting requests to that service. This allows the service time to recover and prevents the failure from propagating through the system. Additionally, retries, timeouts, and fallback mechanisms can be used to improve the system's resilience. Implementing these strategies at the service level can be cumbersome, so many organizations use centralized frameworks like Hystrix or Resilience4j to manage error handling and resilience across multiple services.

Configuration management is another area where cross-cutting concerns must be addressed. As microservices scale and evolve, the configuration of services often changes, and ensuring that each service has the correct configuration at all times can be challenging. Centralized configuration management tools, such as Spring Cloud Config or Consul, can be used to store and manage configuration values in a single location, ensuring that all microservices access the correct configuration settings. These tools also allow for dynamic configuration updates, so changes can be applied to services without requiring them to be redeployed.

Cross-cutting concerns in microservices are fundamental to the architecture's success. From logging and authentication to security, monitoring, and error handling, effectively managing these concerns across multiple services is key to building a robust, scalable system. By leveraging centralized tools and automation, organizations can address these concerns efficiently, allowing microservices to operate independently while maintaining consistency, security, and performance across the entire system. By ensuring that cross-cutting concerns are well-managed, organizations can reduce complexity, improve maintainability, and build microservices systems that are resilient, secure, and capable of scaling to meet the demands of modern applications.

Distributed Transactions in Microservices

In a monolithic architecture, transaction management is relatively straightforward. Typically, a single database holds all the data for the application, and transactions are confined to that database. However, in a microservices architecture, each service usually has its own database, often of a different type, and communicates with other services over the network. This decentralized nature introduces significant complexity when managing transactions that span multiple services. Ensuring data consistency and reliability across services becomes a challenging task, especially when transactions must encompass different data sources or systems. Distributed transactions are the solution to managing transactions across multiple microservices, but they come with their own set of challenges, trade-offs, and best practices.

A distributed transaction in microservices is a transaction that involves more than one service, typically with each service managing its own database. The challenge here is ensuring that all parts of the transaction are successfully completed across services, or that none are, to maintain consistency. In traditional monolithic systems, this is achieved through ACID (Atomicity, Consistency, Isolation, and Durability) transactions within a single database. However, applying ACID principles to microservices is not always feasible due to the inherent distributed nature of the architecture, which requires coordination across multiple databases and services. As a result, distributed transactions in microservices often rely on different approaches and patterns that balance the need for consistency with the need for scalability and resilience.

One of the most widely used patterns for handling distributed transactions in microservices is the Saga pattern. The Saga pattern breaks a large, distributed transaction into a series of smaller, local transactions that are managed by individual microservices. Each local transaction is followed by a compensating action in case something goes wrong. In this way, instead of rolling back a global transaction in the traditional sense, sagas ensure that each microservice can handle its part of the transaction independently and can compensate for failures as necessary. If a failure occurs in any part of the saga, compensating transactions are triggered to undo the changes made by previous services, ensuring that the system as a whole remains consistent.

There are two main types of sagas: choreography-based and orchestration-based. In choreography-based sagas, each service involved in the transaction knows what to do next and communicates directly with other services to continue the flow of the transaction. The services act autonomously, and no central coordinator is required. While this approach can be more scalable and flexible, it can also lead to greater complexity as the number of services grows. On the other hand, orchestration-based sagas use a central service or orchestrator that coordinates the flow of the transaction, sending commands to each service and ensuring that they perform the necessary actions in the correct order. This approach provides more centralized control, which can make it easier to manage the transaction but may also introduce a potential bottleneck or single point of failure.

Another approach to handling distributed transactions in microservices is the use of the two-phase commit (2PC) protocol. This protocol is based on the ACID principles and ensures strong consistency across services. In the first phase, all participants in the transaction are asked to prepare by ensuring that they can commit the changes. If all participants respond positively, the second phase is triggered, and the transaction is committed. If any participant fails to prepare or responds negatively, the transaction is aborted, and all participants roll back their changes. While 2PC guarantees consistency, it can introduce performance bottlenecks and higher latency due to the coordination required between multiple services. It also increases the risk of blocking, as a failure in one service can delay the entire transaction.

Despite the challenges, distributed transactions are crucial for maintaining the integrity of data across multiple microservices. Without an effective strategy for handling distributed transactions, data inconsistencies can arise, leading to incorrect application behavior and potentially significant business risks. Ensuring data consistency in a distributed system is critical in use cases such as financial transactions, inventory management, and order processing, where any inconsistencies could have serious consequences. Distributed transactions provide the mechanisms to ensure that data is consistently updated across all services, even when failures occur.

While the Saga and 2PC patterns are two of the most well-known approaches to distributed transactions in microservices, there are other strategies that may be appropriate depending on the needs of the application. For example, in some cases, an event-driven architecture can be used to manage consistency. In this approach, services communicate via events, and data changes are propagated asynchronously. When a service performs an operation that affects its data, it emits an event that other services listen for. These services can then update their own data stores accordingly. While this approach provides eventual consistency rather than strong consistency, it is often sufficient for applications that can tolerate slight delays in data synchronization. The use of event-driven architectures also enables decoupling between services, reducing the complexity of managing synchronous distributed transactions.

In cases where eventual consistency is acceptable, the application can also rely on techniques such as conflict resolution or data reconciliation. Since distributed transactions in microservices typically involve multiple databases, inconsistencies can occur when data is updated at different times. In such scenarios, a reconciliation process can be put in place to detect and resolve conflicts, ensuring that the system reaches a consistent state over time. This is particularly useful when working with distributed data stores, such as NoSQL databases or event sourcing systems, which prioritize availability and partition tolerance over immediate consistency.

Another critical aspect of handling distributed transactions is the need for robust error handling and fault tolerance. Since microservices are distributed across different environments, they are prone to failures due to network issues, service crashes, or resource constraints. To mitigate these risks, organizations must implement failure detection mechanisms, retries, and timeouts to ensure that transactions are not left incomplete due to transient errors. Additionally, services involved in distributed transactions should be designed with resilience in mind, ensuring that they can recover gracefully from failures and continue to function even in the presence of issues. Circuit breakers, for instance, can help prevent cascading failures by detecting when a service is failing and temporarily halting requests to that service.

Distributed transactions in microservices also require a strong monitoring and observability framework to ensure that the system remains operational and consistent. Since microservices are distributed across multiple services and databases, it can be difficult to track the flow of transactions and detect issues early. Distributed tracing tools like Jaeger or Zipkin, coupled with centralized logging and metrics collection systems like Prometheus and Grafana, can provide real-time insights into the state of transactions and help identify potential issues in the system. Monitoring the health of services, tracking the latency of transactions, and detecting error rates can help organizations quickly pinpoint the source of problems and take corrective actions to prevent data inconsistencies or transaction failures.

Finally, managing distributed transactions in microservices requires careful consideration of the trade-offs between consistency, availability, and performance. In some applications, strong consistency is essential, while in others, eventual consistency may be sufficient. The choice of distributed transaction strategy should be based on the specific requirements of the application and the level of risk associated with potential inconsistencies. By leveraging the right patterns and techniques, such as the Saga pattern, 2PC, or event-driven architectures, organizations can manage distributed transactions effectively, ensuring that microservices can operate autonomously while maintaining data integrity and consistency across the system.

Microservices for Real-Time Systems

In recent years, microservices architecture has gained considerable traction as a way of designing and deploying applications. This approach divides an application into smaller, independent, and loosely coupled services, each responsible for a specific piece of business functionality. Microservices offer numerous benefits such as flexibility, scalability, and resilience. However, when it comes to real-time systems, the microservices architecture presents both opportunities and challenges. Real-time systems demand that data is processed and responded to almost instantaneously. This need for responsiveness requires careful consideration of how microservices interact with each other and how they handle the timely delivery of data across distributed environments. For microservices to be effective in real-time systems, they must be designed with performance, scalability, and responsiveness in mind.

One of the most critical aspects of real-time systems is latency. These systems require the ability to process data and provide responses without significant delays. In a traditional monolithic system, the architecture may be optimized for lower latency, as all components are typically within the same application and access to resources is relatively straightforward. In contrast, microservices introduce more complexity due to their distributed nature. Each service may reside on different servers or containers, and they often communicate over a network, which can introduce latency. For microservices to be effective in real-time systems, it is essential to minimize latency between services. This requires optimizing both the infrastructure and the communication patterns between services.

To minimize latency, it is important to design microservices in such a way that they can process data quickly and efficiently. One approach is to use lightweight communication protocols like gRPC or WebSockets, which are designed for low-latency, high-performance interactions. gRPC, for example, uses Protocol Buffers for serialization, which is much faster and more compact than traditional text-based formats like JSON or XML. Additionally, WebSockets provide a full-duplex communication channel that allows real-time, bidirectional data flow between the client and server, making it ideal for use cases that require constant updates, such as gaming or financial trading platforms.

Event-driven architectures can also play a pivotal role in handling real-time communication in microservices. In a real-time system, microservices often need to respond to events as they occur, such as sensor readings, stock price updates, or user actions. By implementing an event-driven approach, services can listen for specific events and respond as soon as they are triggered. This decouples the components and allows for asynchronous communication, where services do not need to wait for one another to finish processing before continuing. This can significantly reduce latency by ensuring that services can operate in parallel and only focus on the events that are relevant to them. Popular messaging systems like Apache Kafka, RabbitMQ, and NATS are often used in event-driven microservices architectures to handle the communication and coordination of events between services.

In real-time systems, data consistency is often a concern, especially in environments where high throughput and low latency are essential. In a microservices architecture, services typically maintain their own databases, and it is crucial to ensure that these databases remain consistent across the entire system. However, strong consistency models, such as ACID transactions, can introduce latency due to the need to lock resources and perform complex coordination. In real-time systems, achieving consistency in a way that does not impact performance requires careful design. One approach is eventual consistency, where services are allowed to temporarily operate with stale data, with the understanding that they will eventually reach a consistent state. Event sourcing is another pattern commonly used in real-time systems to maintain consistency while allowing services to be decoupled. Event sourcing ensures that every change to the state of an application is captured as an event, allowing services to replay events in order to reach a consistent state without requiring synchronous updates.

Scalability is another essential factor when deploying microservices in real-time systems. Real-time systems often deal with high volumes of data and requests, which require the underlying infrastructure to be scalable in order to handle the load. The ability to scale microservices independently is one of the core advantages of microservices architecture. Each microservice can be scaled based on its individual resource requirements, ensuring that the system can adapt to changes in load without affecting the performance of other services. This is especially important in real-time systems, where traffic patterns can be unpredictable. Kubernetes, a popular container orchestration platform, provides an excellent tool for scaling microservices. Kubernetes can automatically scale services based on predefined metrics, such as CPU or memory usage, and it can also support horizontal scaling by adding or removing instances of a service as demand fluctuates.

Another challenge in real-time systems is ensuring fault tolerance and resilience. In a microservices architecture, the failure of one service should not bring down the entire system. This is especially important in real-time systems, where service interruptions can lead to missed data or delayed responses, negatively impacting the user experience. To ensure resilience, microservices in real-time systems must be designed to fail gracefully. Techniques like circuit breakers, retries, and timeouts can help prevent cascading failures by detecting when a service is unavailable and automatically rerouting requests or attempting the operation again. Furthermore, monitoring and observability are essential to detect issues before they escalate. By leveraging tools like Prometheus, Grafana, or OpenTelemetry, teams can track the health of services in real-time, identify potential bottlenecks, and respond proactively to issues that may affect system performance.

Security is always a critical concern, but in real-time systems, where data is often exchanged rapidly and frequently, securing communications and protecting sensitive information becomes even more crucial. Microservices in real-time systems must implement robust authentication and authorization mechanisms to ensure that only authorized users and services can access specific data or perform certain actions. Token-based authentication systems like OAuth 2.0 and JSON Web Tokens (JWT) are commonly used in microservices architectures to secure communication between services. Additionally, encrypting data in transit using SSL/TLS ensures that sensitive information is not exposed during communication.

In real-time systems, the interaction between users and services is constant and fast. This means that APIs used by microservices must be able to handle a high volume of requests with minimal latency. API gateways are often used to manage and route requests between services, providing a single entry point for all incoming traffic. API gateways can also provide additional functionality such as load balancing, rate limiting, and caching, which can further optimize the performance of microservices in real-time systems. By centralizing common tasks in the API gateway, the microservices themselves can remain focused on their core business logic, improving overall system performance.

Handling real-time interactions in a microservices environment requires careful consideration of various architectural patterns and techniques to ensure low-latency communication, high availability, and resilience. By leveraging event-driven architectures, lightweight communication protocols, and scalable infrastructure, microservices can meet the demands of real-time systems. Additionally, managing data consistency, security, and fault tolerance is crucial for maintaining system reliability and providing an optimal user experience. As real-time systems continue to evolve and demand increases for low-latency applications, the role of microservices in supporting these systems will only become more important, offering the flexibility, scalability, and responsiveness needed to build high-performance, real-time applications.

The Future of Microservices Architecture

Microservices architecture has rapidly become one of the most popular approaches for designing and building applications in the modern software landscape. By breaking down monolithic applications into smaller, independent services, microservices offer numerous advantages, including scalability, flexibility, and ease of deployment. As businesses continue to seek faster innovation cycles and more resilient systems, microservices have proven to be an ideal solution for creating complex, distributed applications. However, as the demand for more advanced, more efficient, and more secure systems grows, the future of microservices architecture is set to evolve. In the coming years, we will see significant changes in how microservices are designed, implemented, and managed, driven by technological advancements, new architectural patterns, and the need to address the challenges of scaling and maintaining increasingly complex systems.

One key aspect of the future of microservices architecture lies in the continued adoption and maturation of containerization technologies, with Kubernetes leading the charge as the standard for container orchestration. As organizations scale their microservices applications, managing containers and services efficiently across distributed environments becomes increasingly complex. Kubernetes has already revolutionized the way containers are deployed, scaled, and managed, but it is expected to continue evolving to meet the demands of more sophisticated microservices architectures. With features like self-healing, automated scaling, and sophisticated networking capabilities, Kubernetes will remain the backbone of modern microservices deployment. In the future, Kubernetes is likely to become even more automated and intelligent, with enhanced support for service discovery, traffic management, and fault tolerance.

Another significant trend that will shape the future of microservices is the increasing reliance on serverless architectures. Serverless computing allows developers to focus more on business logic rather than infrastructure management, as the cloud provider automatically handles the underlying servers and scaling. This paradigm is increasingly attractive for microservices because it further decouples services from the infrastructure and enables fine-grained scaling. Serverless platforms like AWS Lambda, Azure Functions, and Google Cloud Functions are already gaining popularity and will continue to evolve, making it easier to deploy and run microservices without worrying about provisioning or managing servers. In a serverless future, organizations can expect microservices to become even more granular, with a shift toward event-driven architectures that trigger small, stateless functions in response to specific events, further enhancing the flexibility and scalability of applications.

In the future, the interaction between microservices will become even more seamless and efficient with the continued development of service mesh technologies. Service meshes, such as Istio and Linkerd, provide a dedicated infrastructure layer for managing service-to-service communication, offering features like traffic management, security, monitoring, and tracing. As microservices architectures grow in complexity, managing communication between services and ensuring that they can operate securely and efficiently is becoming increasingly difficult. Service meshes are designed to address these challenges by abstracting away the complexities of service-to-service communication, providing a consistent and centralized approach to managing network traffic. Over time, we can expect service meshes to become even more integrated into microservices architectures, with enhanced capabilities for managing traffic, enforcing security policies, and ensuring that services are resilient and responsive.

Security will continue to be a major concern as microservices architectures become more widespread. In a distributed system, securing the communication between services, as well as ensuring that each service is properly authenticated and authorized, presents a significant challenge. As the number of microservices increases, so does the attack surface, making it essential to implement comprehensive security measures. In the future, we are likely to see a greater emphasis on zero-trust security models, where each service is treated as untrusted by default and must authenticate and authorize every request. This model will require enhanced identity management and access controls, as well as automated security policies that adapt to changing conditions. Additionally, microservices architectures will continue to leverage technologies like mutual TLS and API gateways to secure communication between services, ensuring that sensitive data remains protected as it flows between distributed components.

Another important area of growth for microservices in the future is the integration of artificial intelligence (AI) and machine learning (ML) capabilities. As organizations collect more data through their microservices-based applications, the ability to process and analyze this data in real time becomes crucial. AI and ML can be used to improve the performance and efficiency of microservices by enabling them to make intelligent decisions based on the data they process. For instance, microservices could be equipped with predictive capabilities that help optimize service routing, load balancing, or resource allocation. In addition, AI-powered monitoring tools can automatically detect and resolve issues in real time, reducing the need for manual intervention. The integration of AI and ML into microservices architectures will unlock new opportunities for automation, performance optimization, and smarter decision-making across distributed applications.

As microservices architecture continues to evolve, developers will also benefit from increasingly sophisticated tools for managing and maintaining these complex systems. The future of microservices will likely see the emergence of more advanced DevOps and CI/CD (continuous integration/continuous deployment) practices that allow for faster, more efficient development cycles. These practices will be supported by automated testing, deployment, and monitoring tools that can seamlessly integrate with the microservices infrastructure. Additionally, as microservices environments grow in scale, observability will become even more important. Developers will need better visibility into the health and performance of their services to detect and troubleshoot issues quickly. In the future, we can expect more advanced observability tools that provide deep insights into the inner workings of microservices, offering better tracing, logging, and real-time monitoring capabilities.

One of the challenges of microservices architecture is the complexity of managing and orchestrating large numbers of services. As the number of microservices increases, the difficulty of coordinating them, ensuring they communicate properly, and maintaining consistency across the system grows exponentially. To address this challenge, we are likely to see greater integration of artificial intelligence and automation into the management and orchestration of microservices. In the future, platforms like Kubernetes and service meshes will leverage machine learning algorithms to automatically optimize service placement, manage traffic, and ensure that services are resilient. These platforms may also be able to predict and resolve issues before they occur, further improving the efficiency and reliability of microservices-based applications.

The future of microservices architecture will also be shaped by advancements in hybrid and multi-cloud environments. As businesses continue to adopt cloud technologies, many will choose to deploy microservices across multiple clouds or on-premise infrastructures to avoid vendor lock-in, optimize performance, and meet specific regulatory requirements. This hybrid and multi-cloud approach will require enhanced tools and frameworks to manage the deployment, scaling, and monitoring of microservices across diverse environments. Expect to see better integration of microservices platforms with public and private clouds, as well as more sophisticated multi-cloud orchestration capabilities that allow for seamless management of services across various cloud providers.

As microservices evolve, they will become more specialized and optimized for specific use cases. This specialization will allow for even greater efficiency and performance, enabling organizations to meet the demands of more complex and dynamic applications. In the future, we may see microservices built specifically for particular industries or functions, such as finance, healthcare, or IoT, allowing organizations to take advantage of highly optimized services tailored to their needs. These specialized services will integrate seamlessly with other microservices, offering organizations the flexibility to build customized applications while benefiting from the scalability and resilience that microservices provide.

In the years to come, microservices will continue to evolve, driven by technological advancements, growing organizational needs, and the demand for greater efficiency, security, and scalability. The future of microservices architecture will see even greater integration with AI, improved security models, more sophisticated orchestration and management tools, and a continued push toward specialization and automation. As microservices become more advanced and pervasive, organizations will have the ability to build even more resilient, scalable, and intelligent applications that meet the demands of a fast-paced digital world.

Microservices in the Internet of Things (IoT)

The Internet of Things (IoT) is rapidly transforming the way we interact with the world around us. It connects everyday objects to the internet, allowing them to collect and exchange data, providing unprecedented opportunities for automation, monitoring, and optimization across various industries, from manufacturing to healthcare. As the IoT ecosystem grows, so does the complexity of managing the vast amount of data generated by IoT devices. This is where microservices architecture comes into play. Microservices break down applications into smaller, independent services, each responsible for a specific task. This approach is ideal for IoT systems, where multiple devices generate large amounts of data, and where each device may have different requirements for data processing, storage, and communication. By leveraging microservices, IoT systems can achieve scalability, flexibility, and maintainability, which are essential as the number of connected devices continues to grow.

One of the most significant challenges in IoT systems is handling the massive volume of data generated by sensors, devices, and applications. Traditional monolithic architectures often struggle to scale in such environments because they rely on centralized databases and processes that can become bottlenecks. In contrast, microservices architectures allow for the distribution of data processing and storage across multiple services, enabling more efficient handling of large data streams. Each microservice can be tailored to handle specific tasks such as data collection, storage, analysis, or communication with external systems. This distribution of responsibility makes it easier to scale the system and adapt to the changing demands of the IoT environment.

For example, a smart home system may consist of multiple devices such as smart thermostats, lights, and security cameras, each generating data that needs to be processed and stored. Instead of relying on a single monolithic application to manage all these devices, a microservices architecture can divide the system into smaller services. One microservice could handle communication with the thermostat, another could process video streams from the security cameras, and yet another could store user preferences and historical data. This division of labor ensures that each component can be optimized for its specific task, and it allows the system to scale efficiently as the number of devices increases.

Microservices are also ideal for enabling real-time data processing in IoT systems. In many IoT applications, such as industrial automation or healthcare monitoring, real-time data processing is crucial. For example, in a smart factory, sensors attached to machines may continuously monitor temperature, pressure, and other parameters.

Microservices can be used to process this data in real time, triggering alerts or taking automated actions when certain thresholds are exceeded. Each microservice can be responsible for a particular aspect of real-time processing, such as filtering raw data, analyzing trends, or triggering notifications. By using microservices, organizations can ensure that each piece of data is processed efficiently and that the system can respond to events as they happen.

Furthermore, microservices enable greater flexibility in handling diverse IoT devices and protocols. IoT devices come in many different shapes and sizes, and they communicate using a variety of protocols such as MQTT, CoAP, or HTTP. Each device may require different handling based on its capabilities, communication protocol, and the type of data it generates. Microservices make it easier to accommodate these differences by allowing each service to interact with specific types of devices or protocols. For example, one microservice could be responsible for handling devices that communicate via MQTT, while another could handle devices that use HTTP. This approach decouples the communication logic from the core business logic, making it easier to add new devices or protocols to the system without disrupting the entire architecture.

The scalability of microservices is also a key advantage in IoT systems. As the number of connected devices grows, so does the amount of data and the need for processing power. Traditional monolithic systems often struggle to scale efficiently, as increasing load on one part of the system can lead to performance degradation across the entire application. Microservices, on the other hand, can be independently scaled to meet the demands of specific components. For example, if a particular microservice responsible for processing sensor data is receiving a large influx of data, it can be scaled up by adding more instances of that service without affecting the other parts of the system. This ensures that the system can handle the growing demands of an expanding IoT network.

Another key benefit of microservices in IoT systems is fault tolerance. In a monolithic architecture, a failure in one part of the system can often bring down the entire application. In contrast, microservices are designed to be resilient and fault-tolerant. Each microservice operates independently, so if one service fails, the rest of the system can continue to function. This is particularly important in IoT applications where devices and services are distributed across different locations and environments. A failure in one part of the system should not cause the entire IoT network to collapse. By using techniques such as service redundancy, health checks, and automatic retries, microservices can ensure that the system remains operational even in the face of individual service failures.

Security is also a critical consideration in IoT systems, as many IoT devices handle sensitive data and are vulnerable to attacks. Microservices can enhance security by allowing for more granular control over access to specific services. For example, each microservice can have its own set of security policies, such as authentication and authorization rules, ensuring that only authorized devices and users can access certain parts of the system. Additionally, because microservices are often deployed in isolated containers, they provide a more secure environment for running IoT applications compared to traditional monolithic systems. Each microservice can be secured independently, reducing the attack surface and ensuring that vulnerabilities in one part of the system do not affect other services.

In an IoT environment, it is crucial to ensure that services can be updated and maintained without causing disruption to the entire system. Microservices make it easier to achieve continuous integration and continuous deployment (CI/CD) in IoT systems. With microservices, individual services can be updated or replaced without affecting the rest of the system. For example, if a new version of a service that processes sensor data is released, it can be deployed independently, and the system can continue to function without downtime. This allows for more frequent updates and quicker response times to issues or feature requests, which is essential in fast-moving IoT environments where new devices and protocols are constantly being introduced.

The ability to integrate with other systems and platforms is another advantage of using microservices in IoT applications. IoT devices often need to communicate with external systems, such as cloud services, enterprise applications, or third-party APIs. Microservices make it easier to integrate these external systems by providing well-defined APIs that allow for seamless communication. For example, an IoT system that monitors environmental conditions in a building can send data to a cloud platform for storage and analysis. Microservices can handle the integration with the cloud platform, ensuring that data is transmitted securely and efficiently.

Microservices also make it easier to implement advanced analytics and machine learning (ML) capabilities in IoT systems. As IoT devices generate vast amounts of data, organizations can leverage microservices to process, analyze, and store this data in real time. Machine learning models can be deployed as microservices that analyze data from IoT devices and provide insights or predictions. This allows organizations to make data-driven decisions and optimize their IoT systems based on the insights generated by these models. For example, in a smart factory, microservices could be used to predict equipment failures based on sensor data, enabling proactive maintenance and reducing downtime.

In the rapidly growing world of IoT, microservices provide the scalability, flexibility, and resilience needed to support complex, distributed systems. By breaking down IoT applications into smaller, independent services, microservices enable more efficient processing, real-time responsiveness, and easier integration with other systems. With their ability to scale, handle diverse protocols, and maintain high availability, microservices are well-suited to the demands of modern IoT environments. As the number of connected devices continues to grow, microservices will play an increasingly vital role in managing and optimizing the vast amounts of data generated by IoT devices, enabling more intelligent, secure, and efficient systems.

Using Microservices for Mobile Application Backends

In today's mobile-first world, applications are an integral part of daily life. With millions of mobile apps available, delivering high-performance, scalable, and reliable applications is crucial. To meet these demands, many developers are turning to microservices architecture for mobile application backends. Microservices, which divide applications into small, independent services that each handle a specific business function, offer significant advantages over traditional monolithic architectures, particularly for mobile apps that require agility, scalability, and fast development cycles. Microservices enable mobile application backends to handle a wide range of tasks from user authentication to data storage, API integrations, and business logic processing, all while maintaining flexibility and resilience as the mobile app evolves.

One of the key reasons why microservices are ideal for mobile application backends is scalability. As mobile applications grow in popularity, their backend services must be able to scale effectively to accommodate an increasing number of users and devices. Traditional monolithic architectures often face limitations when scaling, as the entire application needs to be scaled as a single unit, which can lead to inefficiencies and resource constraints. With microservices, each service can be scaled independently based on its specific requirements. For example, a mobile app that experiences a sudden increase in user traffic for one feature, such as a payment service or a social feed, can scale only the relevant service rather than the entire backend. This ability to scale individual services independently ensures that resources are used efficiently, and the mobile app backend can handle large volumes of traffic without affecting overall performance.

In addition to scalability, microservices also enable flexibility in mobile application backends. Mobile applications often need to evolve rapidly in response to changing user demands, new feature requests, or external integrations. Microservices make it easier to modify and update individual components of the backend without affecting the entire system. For instance, if the mobile app introduces a new feature, such as push notifications, developers can create a separate microservice to handle notifications without interfering with other services like user management or data storage. This modularity allows developers to work on different components simultaneously, speeding up the development process and making it easier to iterate on new features. It also simplifies the process of adopting new technologies or changing third-party integrations. If a mobile app needs to switch from one payment gateway to another, for example, the payment microservice can be replaced without impacting other parts of the system.

Reliability and fault tolerance are crucial for any backend system, especially for mobile applications, where downtime or slow performance can significantly affect user experience. Microservices architecture inherently supports resilience by isolating faults. If one service fails, the rest of the application can continue to function, ensuring that users can still interact with other parts of the app. For instance, if a user's profile service experiences issues, they may still be able to browse other sections of the app, such as the news feed or marketplace. Microservices also facilitate the implementation of fault tolerance strategies such as retries, circuit breakers, and graceful degradation. This makes it easier to build a robust backend that can continue operating under adverse conditions, improving the overall reliability of the mobile application.

Another advantage of using microservices for mobile application backends is the ability to handle various types of data and workloads effectively. Mobile applications typically generate a wide variety of data, from user interactions to media uploads, location data, and device information. Each type of data may have different processing, storage, and security requirements. Microservices allow developers to design specific services that are optimized for handling particular data types. For example, a mobile app with media-sharing features can have a dedicated microservice for processing images and videos, which may require different storage and caching strategies than user profile data. By separating these concerns into independent services, the backend can be optimized for each workload, improving performance and scalability.

Moreover, microservices enable improved security and access control in mobile application backends. Since each service is isolated, developers can enforce strict security measures for each individual microservice. For example, user authentication and authorization can be handled by a dedicated authentication service, which can manage login credentials, tokens, and access control across different parts of the app. This isolation helps prevent security breaches from spreading throughout the entire backend, reducing the impact of potential vulnerabilities. Additionally, microservices facilitate the adoption of modern authentication protocols such as OAuth 2.0, OpenID Connect, and JSON Web Tokens (JWT), making it easier to integrate secure authentication mechanisms into the mobile app.

API design is a critical aspect of mobile application backends, as mobile apps rely heavily on APIs to communicate with backend services. Microservices architecture naturally lends itself to API-driven development, as each microservice typically exposes a well-defined API that other services or the mobile app can interact with. This API-first approach allows for better API management, versioning, and documentation. Each microservice's API can be optimized for performance, ensuring that data is transmitted efficiently between the mobile app and the backend. For instance, if a mobile app needs to fetch a user's profile information, the user service's API will return the necessary data in a lightweight format such as JSON, ensuring fast and efficient communication. Additionally, by using technologies like GraphQL or RESTful APIs, microservices can provide flexible, scalable, and secure data access patterns that are ideal for mobile applications.

Microservices also support continuous delivery and deployment (CI/CD) practices, which are essential for modern mobile application development. With the rapid pace of change in mobile applications, frequent updates and bug fixes are often necessary. Microservices make it easier to implement CI/CD pipelines, where each service can be developed, tested, and deployed independently. This allows for faster development cycles and more frequent releases without risking downtime or disruption to the entire application. Each microservice can go through its own set of automated tests, ensuring that new features or fixes do not break existing functionality. Additionally, microservices support blue-green deployments and canary releases, where updates can be deployed gradually and safely, minimizing the risk of introducing errors or issues into the production environment.

In mobile application backends, managing user sessions and interactions across different devices and platforms can be challenging. Microservices help address this challenge by allowing developers to design stateless services that do not rely on any persistent session data. This stateless approach means that mobile apps can interact with any service at any time, and the backend does not need to maintain a session state. If a user switches devices, for instance, the backend can continue to operate as usual, enabling a seamless user experience across multiple platforms. Stateless services can also scale more effectively, as they do not need to store session data, allowing for better resource utilization.

Despite all these advantages, managing a microservices-based backend for mobile applications can also introduce new challenges. Developers need to manage service discovery, communication, data consistency, and monitoring across multiple services. This can become complex as the number of services grows, and it requires robust tools and practices to ensure that the system operates smoothly. Tools like Kubernetes for orchestration, Prometheus for monitoring, and service meshes like Istio can help manage and monitor microservices at scale. Additionally, it is important to design microservices with proper fault tolerance and error handling to ensure that the backend can continue to function under high loads or in the event of service failures.

Using microservices for mobile application backends provides numerous advantages in terms of scalability, flexibility, security, and maintainability. Microservices allow developers to break down complex applications into manageable, independent components, each optimized for a specific task. This enables efficient handling of user data, device communication, and real-time processing, while also ensuring that the backend can scale effectively as the app grows. With the right tools and practices in place, microservices can help developers build high-performance, resilient, and secure mobile applications that can meet the demands of today's mobile-first world. As mobile applications continue to evolve, the role of microservices in powering their backends will only become more critical, allowing for faster innovation and more seamless user experiences.

Scaling Microservices with Horizontal and Vertical Scaling

Scaling is a fundamental requirement for any modern application, particularly for microservices architectures. As organizations deploy microservices to handle diverse business functions, the need to scale these services in response to growing user demands, increasing data volumes, or performance requirements becomes essential. Microservices offer flexibility when it comes to scaling, as they enable both horizontal and vertical scaling strategies. Both of these scaling approaches have their advantages, limitations, and appropriate use cases, and understanding how to apply them effectively is key to ensuring that a microservices architecture can meet the evolving demands of a growing system.

Horizontal scaling, also known as scaling out, involves adding more instances of a service to distribute the load across multiple machines or containers. This is perhaps the most common form of scaling in microservices architectures because it aligns well with the distributed, decoupled nature of microservices. By scaling services horizontally, organizations can handle increased traffic and ensure high availability by balancing requests across multiple service instances. When one instance becomes overwhelmed or fails, traffic can be rerouted to other healthy instances, maintaining the overall performance of the system. Horizontal scaling is particularly effective for stateless services, which do not rely on session-specific data stored locally on a single instance. Since these services do not maintain state, any instance can process requests independently, making it easy to distribute the load evenly across many instances.

For instance, consider a microservice responsible for handling user authentication in a high-traffic web application. As the number of users grows, a single instance of this service may not be sufficient to handle the increased load. Horizontal scaling enables the deployment of additional instances of the authentication service, distributing the requests across multiple servers. Load balancers, which can be either software-based or hardware-based, can be used to direct incoming requests to the least-loaded instance of the service, ensuring that no single instance is overwhelmed. Additionally, by using container orchestration platforms like Kubernetes, horizontal scaling can be automated, with new instances of a service being spun up or down based on traffic demands, ensuring optimal resource utilization.

Horizontal scaling also offers the advantage of fault tolerance. When a service instance fails or becomes unresponsive, the system can continue functioning by rerouting requests to other healthy instances. This ensures that the application remains available and responsive even in the face of individual service failures. Moreover, because new instances can be spun up quickly, horizontal scaling supports rapid scaling in response to sudden traffic spikes, making it ideal for applications that experience fluctuating or unpredictable demand.

On the other hand, vertical scaling, or scaling up, involves increasing the resources of a single instance by adding more CPU, memory, or storage. Vertical scaling is typically used for stateful services or workloads that require more processing power, such as data-intensive applications or services that handle complex computations. While horizontal scaling distributes the load across multiple instances, vertical scaling increases the capacity of a single service instance to handle a higher load. This can be an attractive option for applications that are difficult to decouple into smaller, independent services or that require centralized data processing.

For example, consider a microservice that performs intensive data analytics or machine learning tasks. These tasks may require large amounts of memory and CPU resources that cannot easily be distributed across multiple instances. In such cases, vertical scaling may be necessary to increase the power of a single instance to handle the computational load. Vertical scaling allows the service to process larger datasets or handle more requests without the need for re-architecting the system. It is often easier to implement in the short term for services that need additional resources, as it may only involve upgrading the hardware or adjusting resource allocation within a cloud environment.

However, vertical scaling has its limitations. While it may offer a quick solution to resource constraints, it is not as flexible or scalable as horizontal scaling. There is a physical limit to how much a single machine or instance can be scaled up. Eventually, the system will reach a point where adding more resources to a single instance will no longer be cost-effective or technically feasible. This makes vertical scaling more suitable for applications with relatively stable or predictable workloads that do not require the elasticity and fault tolerance offered by horizontal scaling.

The choice between horizontal and vertical scaling depends on the specific requirements of the service, workload, and the overall architecture of the system. In many cases, a hybrid approach combining both horizontal and vertical scaling may be the most effective. For example, stateless microservices that handle user requests or messaging can be scaled horizontally to handle fluctuating demand, while stateful services that require significant computational resources can be scaled vertically to ensure that they have the capacity to handle large workloads. By combining both approaches, organizations can achieve the benefits of both horizontal and vertical scaling, optimizing resource utilization while ensuring that the system can handle varying loads and meet performance requirements.

In microservices architectures, scaling is not just about adding more resources or instances; it also involves ensuring that the system can scale efficiently. Microservices should be designed with scalability in mind, ensuring that they are loosely coupled, stateless where possible, and capable of handling increased traffic without significant changes to the overall system. For example, databases should be partitioned or sharded to distribute the data across multiple nodes, allowing the system to scale horizontally without running into performance bottlenecks. Similarly, APIs should be designed to be stateless, enabling services to scale independently and allowing the system to accommodate changes in demand.

Automation plays a critical role in scaling microservices efficiently. Cloud platforms and container orchestration tools like Kubernetes provide robust support for automatically scaling microservices. Kubernetes can automatically scale services based on predefined metrics, such as CPU usage, memory usage, or custom application-specific metrics. This allows microservices to scale up or down dynamically in response to real-time demand. Additionally, Kubernetes' Horizontal Pod Autoscaling feature enables automatic scaling of microservices based on traffic patterns, ensuring that resources are allocated efficiently and that services are always available to meet demand.

The orchestration of scaling strategies is also critical. When scaling microservices, it is important to ensure that the dependencies between services are managed effectively. For example, a service that handles customer orders may depend on another service that manages inventory. When scaling the order service horizontally, it is important to ensure that the inventory service can scale appropriately as well, so that inventory updates are processed correctly across all instances. Service meshes, such as Istio, provide a way to manage service-to-service communication and ensure that traffic is routed to the appropriate instances, even as services are scaled dynamically.

Scaling microservices through both horizontal and vertical strategies allows organizations to meet the demands of modern, high-performance applications. Horizontal scaling provides the flexibility to handle unpredictable traffic patterns, ensuring that services remain responsive and fault-tolerant, while vertical scaling allows services to take advantage of additional resources when needed. By leveraging both scaling methods, combined with automation and effective orchestration, organizations can build microservices architectures that can handle increased traffic, evolving workloads, and future growth while ensuring optimal performance and reliability.

Microservices and Machine Learning Integration

The integration of machine learning (ML) into modern software architectures is increasingly becoming a key driver of innovation across industries. Machine learning enables systems to predict outcomes, optimize processes, and make decisions based on data, all of which are essential for businesses to stay competitive. As the need for scalable, flexible, and maintainable architectures grows, microservices have become an ideal choice for deploying machine learning models. Microservices, which break down applications into smaller, independently deployable services, offer a flexible, decentralized approach to integrating machine learning in ways that promote scalability, speed, and operational efficiency. This integration, however, introduces unique challenges and requires thoughtful design decisions to ensure that machine learning models are seamlessly incorporated into microservices-based systems.

Machine learning models are typically computationally intensive and often require specialized infrastructure and resources to train and deploy effectively. Microservices architecture provides an elegant solution to managing these demands by isolating different components of the machine learning pipeline, allowing each microservice to be responsible for a specific task. For example, one microservice could handle data collection and preprocessing, another could manage the training of machine learning models, while others could focus on the deployment and real-time inference. This segmentation of tasks allows each microservice to be optimized for its particular function and enables teams to scale parts of the ML pipeline independently, without overburdening any single component. Furthermore, the ability to update and deploy microservices independently of each other allows for rapid iteration and optimization of machine learning models, which is crucial in environments where continuous improvement is required.

One of the main advantages of using microservices for machine learning is the ability to scale components independently. Machine learning models, especially deep learning models, can require significant computational resources during both training and inference phases. With microservices, organizations can scale the components that need more computational power, such as training microservices, without affecting other parts of the system. For example, during the training phase, microservices responsible for training the model can be deployed on machines with high-performance GPUs or TPUs to accelerate the learning process. After training, the model can be deployed in inference microservices, which can be scaled horizontally to handle large numbers of prediction requests. By using horizontal scaling, organizations can handle spikes in demand for real-time predictions without affecting the performance of other services.

In a machine learning pipeline, data preprocessing and feature engineering are crucial steps that require significant computational resources and data handling. These tasks can be broken down into separate microservices, each focused on a specific aspect of the data pipeline. For instance, one microservice could be dedicated to cleaning and filtering raw data, while another might focus on feature extraction and transformation. By breaking the data pipeline into smaller microservices, each service can be optimized for a specific task and scaled independently based on the amount of data being processed. This separation allows for better resource utilization and ensures that the machine learning pipeline can handle growing amounts of data without performance degradation.

Integrating machine learning models into a microservices architecture also facilitates the deployment and serving of models in a flexible, scalable way. Once a machine learning model is trained, it is often packaged as a service and deployed to handle real-time predictions.

Microservices can expose APIs that allow other services or applications to send data to the model for predictions. For example, a fraud detection model in a microservices-based payment application could be served as a separate service that receives payment transaction data, applies the trained model, and returns the prediction of whether the transaction is fraudulent. This decoupling of the model from the rest of the application makes it easier to manage, update, and scale the ML model without affecting other parts of the system. Additionally, the separation of the model into its own service enables multiple applications to share and use the model, enhancing its accessibility and promoting reuse across different business units or use cases.

In addition to scaling and modularity, microservices architecture enables continuous deployment and integration (CI/CD) practices, which are critical for machine learning workflows. In traditional software systems, CI/CD practices focus on automating the build, testing, and deployment of code. However, machine learning workflows often involve different complexities, such as model retraining, hyperparameter tuning, and versioning. With microservices, these tasks can be automated and streamlined as part of the overall CI/CD pipeline. For instance, a dedicated microservice can periodically check for new data and trigger the retraining of a model, while another service can manage the deployment of new model versions into production. This continuous cycle of retraining, testing, and deployment ensures that machine learning models remain up-to-date and can adapt to changing data patterns over time.

Another benefit of using microservices in ML integration is the ability to experiment with different models or algorithms without affecting the overall system. Because each machine learning model is deployed as an independent service, it is possible to test multiple versions of a model in parallel, compare their performance, and select the best-performing model. This is especially useful in scenarios where organizations want to compare various machine learning algorithms or approaches to determine which provides the best results for a specific use case. A/B testing or canary releases can be used to serve different models to different user groups, ensuring that the new model can be tested in a live environment before full deployment. This capability promotes faster innovation and experimentation, which is essential in dynamic, data-driven industries.

Microservices can also facilitate the management of machine learning models in production. ML models are often subject to degradation over time due to changes in data patterns, a phenomenon known as model drift. Microservices enable organizations to monitor the performance of models in real time, detect signs of model drift, and retrain or replace models when necessary. Monitoring tools and logging can be integrated into the microservices to track model performance and trigger actions like model retraining or alerting system administrators to performance issues. This ensures that machine learning models remain accurate and reliable, which is critical in fields like healthcare, finance, and autonomous systems, where outdated or inaccurate models can lead to serious consequences.

However, integrating machine learning into microservices architecture does introduce challenges. Managing and orchestrating the communication between numerous microservices can become complex, especially as the number of services and models increases. Efficient management of model storage, versioning, and access is another challenge, particularly when multiple models are being used across various applications or services. Additionally, ensuring that each microservice has access to the necessary computational resources, such as GPUs or specialized hardware, can require careful configuration and management. Tools like Kubernetes, which supports the orchestration of containerized microservices, can help streamline the management of resources, deployments, and scaling, but it still requires expertise to configure and maintain.

Despite these challenges, the benefits of using microservices for machine learning integration far outweigh the potential drawbacks. By leveraging microservices, organizations can achieve scalable, flexible, and maintainable machine learning systems that can adapt to evolving data, rapidly deploy new models, and scale independently based on demand. The decoupled nature of microservices allows for a modular, efficient, and secure architecture for deploying machine learning models, enabling organizations to fully realize the potential of their machine learning investments while maintaining agility and resilience.

Case Studies in Microservices: Success and Failure Stories

Microservices have revolutionized how applications are designed, deployed, and maintained. By breaking down monolithic systems into smaller, independently deployable services, microservices architecture offers improved scalability, flexibility, and resilience. However, the adoption of microservices is not without its challenges. Over the years, several companies have embraced this architectural style, experiencing both remarkable success and significant failures. Case studies of these real-world applications offer valuable lessons about the benefits, risks, and best practices of microservices, providing insight into how this architecture can be implemented effectively or lead to unintended consequences.

One of the most prominent success stories in microservices adoption is that of Netflix. The streaming giant is often cited as a prime example of how microservices can enable a business to scale efficiently and remain resilient. In the early days, Netflix operated on a monolithic architecture that became difficult to scale and maintain as the company grew. The shift to microservices allowed Netflix to break down its application into hundreds of smaller services, each focused on a specific business function, such as user authentication, content recommendation, or streaming. This modularity enabled Netflix to scale each service independently based on demand, allowing the platform to handle millions of concurrent users without compromising performance.

One of the key factors behind Netflix's success with microservices is the company's emphasis on automation. Netflix relies heavily on automated testing, continuous delivery, and deployment to ensure that new features or updates can be pushed to production without affecting the stability of the platform. Additionally, the company invested in robust monitoring and observability tools to gain insights into the health of each microservice. By using tools like Chaos Monkey, which deliberately causes failures in the system to test resilience, Netflix can quickly identify vulnerabilities and ensure that the system remains operational under adverse conditions. This approach has helped

Netflix maintain high availability, even during peak traffic periods like the release of new popular shows or movies.

Similarly, Uber's adoption of microservices has enabled it to scale its operations globally. Originally, Uber relied on a monolithic architecture, but as the number of users and drivers grew, the system became more difficult to manage. By transitioning to microservices, Uber was able to decompose its application into smaller services that could be independently deployed, scaled, and maintained. This shift allowed Uber to optimize its system to handle various aspects of the business, from ride requests and payments to mapping and driver coordination. The ability to scale individual services has been particularly beneficial for Uber in handling fluctuations in demand, ensuring that the app remains responsive during peak times, such as rush hours or special events.

One of Uber's key strategies for success with microservices is the use of APIs and event-driven architecture to ensure seamless communication between services. Uber relies on message queues and event brokers like Kafka to enable asynchronous communication between microservices, ensuring that services do not become tightly coupled. This decoupling allows Uber to iterate quickly and deploy new features without disrupting the entire system. Additionally, the company has invested in robust fault tolerance and recovery mechanisms, allowing it to quickly address any issues that arise without compromising service availability.

While there are many success stories in microservices adoption, there are also notable failures that highlight the challenges of this architecture. One such example is the experience of Twitter. In the early years of its operation, Twitter relied on a monolithic architecture that struggled to handle the growing traffic from millions of users. The company made the decision to shift to a microservices-based architecture in hopes of improving scalability and performance. However, Twitter's transition was not smooth, and the company faced significant challenges during the migration.

One of the main problems Twitter encountered was the complexity of managing the numerous microservices. As the number of services increased, so did the difficulty of managing inter-service communication, monitoring, and debugging. Twitter struggled with issues like service dependencies, network latency, and data consistency across services. The lack of a clear strategy for managing distributed systems led to service failures and performance bottlenecks, and the company spent years working to stabilize its infrastructure. In hindsight, Twitter's experience highlights the importance of proper planning, monitoring, and error handling when adopting microservices. While microservices can provide significant benefits, organizations must be prepared for the added complexity of managing distributed systems at scale.

Another example of failure in microservices adoption is that of a large e-commerce company, which attempted to transition to a microservices architecture to improve flexibility and scalability. Initially, the company saw some benefits from the transition, such as the ability to develop and deploy new features more quickly. However, as the company added more microservices to its infrastructure, it began to experience significant challenges in maintaining the system. The team found it increasingly difficult to keep track of dependencies between services, and frequent communication issues between microservices led to outages and downtime.

One of the critical problems the e-commerce company faced was a lack of clear ownership and governance over the various microservices. Different teams were responsible for different services, but there was no centralized strategy for managing them. This lack of coordination led to inconsistent development practices, which made it difficult to maintain system reliability. Additionally, the company struggled with data consistency and ensuring that transactions were properly handled across services. As a result, the benefits of microservices were overshadowed by the operational difficulties, and the company eventually reverted to a more monolithic architecture for some critical parts of its system. This failure serves as a reminder that while microservices offer flexibility, they also require a strong commitment to governance, monitoring, and service management.

These case studies underscore the importance of careful planning and execution when adopting microservices. Companies like Netflix and Uber have successfully leveraged microservices to scale their operations and improve system resilience, but their success is rooted in automation, continuous testing, robust monitoring, and a strong commitment to fault tolerance. On the other hand, companies like Twitter and the e-commerce business faced significant challenges because they underestimated the complexity of managing distributed systems, the importance of inter-service communication, and the need for clear governance over the various microservices.

The key takeaway from these case studies is that microservices are not a one-size-fits-all solution. While they offer numerous advantages, such as improved scalability and faster development cycles, they also introduce complexity that requires a disciplined approach to architecture, development, and operations. Companies must be prepared for the challenges of managing a distributed system and ensure they have the necessary tools and processes in place to monitor, secure, and maintain the various microservices. By learning from both success stories and failures, organizations can make more informed decisions about when and how to adopt microservices, ensuring they can harness the full potential of this architectural style.

www.ingramcontent.com/pod-product-compliance
Lightning Source LLC
LaVergne TN
LVHW051231050326
832903LV00028B/2340